DIABLO™

THE OFFICIAL STRATEGY GUIDE

NOW AVAILABLE FROM PRIMA

Computer Game Books

1942: The Pacific Air War—The Official Strategy Guide
The 11th Hour: The Official Strategy Guide
The 7th Guest: The Official Strategy Guide
A-Train: the Official Strategy Guide
Aces Over Europe: The Official Strategy Guide
Across the Rhine: The Official Strategy Guide
Aegis: Guardian of the Fleet - The Official Strategy Guide
Alone in the Dark 3: The Official Strategy Guide
Alone in the Dark: The Official Strategy Guide
Armored Fist: The Official Strategy Guide
Angel Devoid: The Official Strategy Guide
Armored Fist: The Official Strategy Guide
Ascendancy: The Official Strategy Guide
Betrayal at Krondor: The Official Strategy Guide
Blackthorne: The Official Strategy Guide
Buried in Time: The Journeyman Project 2—The Official Strategy Guide
CD-ROM Unauthorized Game Secrets, Volume 2
CD-ROM Classics
Caesar II: The Official Strategy Guide
Celtic Tales: Balor of the Evil Eye—The Official Strategy Guide
Chuck Yeager's Air Combat Strategy
Civilization II The Official Strategy Guide
Cyberia: The Official Strategy Guide
Cyberia^2 Resurrection: The Official Strategy Guide
Dark Seed II: The Official Strategy Guide
Descent: The Official Strategy Guide
Descent II: The Official Strategy Guide
DOOM Battlebook
DOOM II: The Official Strategy Guide
Dracula Unleashed: The Official Strategy Guide and Novel
Dragon Lore: The Official Strategy Guide
Dungeon Master II: The Legend of Skullkeep—The Official Strategy Guide
Empire Deluxe: The Official Strategy Guide
Fleet Defender: The Official Strategy Guide
Frankenstein: Through the Eyes of the Monster—The Official Strategy Guide
Front Page Sports Baseball '94: The Official Playbook
Front Page Sports Football Pro '95: The Official Playbook
Fury^3: The Official Strategy Guide
Harpoon II: The Official Strategy Guide
Hell: A Cyberpunk Thriller—The Official Strategy Guide
Heretic: The Official Strategy Guide
I Have No Mouth and I Must Scream: The Official Strategy Guide
In The 1st Degree: The Official Strategy Guide
Kingdom: The Far Reaches—The Official Strategy Guide
King's Quest VII: The Unauthorized Strategy Guide
Klik & Plaly 1.0: The Official Strategy Guide
The Legend of Kyrandia: The Official Strategy Guide
Lode Runner: The Legend Returns—Official Guide . . .
Lords of Midnight: The Official Strategy Guide
Machiavelli the Prince: Official Secrets & Solutions
Marathon: The Official Strategy Guide
Master of Orion: The Official Strategy Guide
Master of Magic: The Official Strategy Guide
Mech Warrior 2: The Official Strategy Guide
Mech Warrior 2 Expansion Pack Secrets and Solutions

Microsoft Arcade: The Official Strategy Guide
Microsoft Flight Simulator 5.1: The Official Strategy Guide
Microsoft Golf: The Official Strategy Guide
Microsoft Golf 2: The Official Strategy Guide
Microsoft Space Simulator: The Official Strategy Guide
Might and Magic Compendium:
    The Authorized Strategy Guide for Games I, II, III, and IV
Mission Critical: The Official Strategy Guide
Myst: The Official Strategy Guide, Revised Edition
The Official Lucasfilm Games Air Combat Strategies Book
Online Games: In-Depth Strategies and Secrets
Oregon Trail II: The Official Strategy Guide
Outpost: The Official Strategy Guide
Pagan: Ultima VIII - the Ultimate Strategy Guide
The Pagemaster Official CD-ROM Strategy Guide and Companion
Panzer General: The Official Strategy Guide
Perfect General II: The Official Strategy Guide
Populous: The Official Strategy Guide
Power Pete: Official Secrets & Solutions
Powerhouse Official Secrets & Solutions
Prima's Playstation Game Secrets: The Unauthorized Strategy Guide
Prince of Persia: The Official Strategy Guide
Prisoner of Ice: The Official Strategy Guide
Quest for Glory: The Authorized Strategy Guide
The Residents: Bad Day on the Midway—The Official Strategy Guide
Return to Zork Adventurer's Guide
Ripper: The Official Strategy Guide
Romance of the Three Kingdoms IV: Wall of Fire—The Official Strategy Guide
Shadow of the Comet: The Official Strategy Guide
Shannara: The Official Strategy Guide
Sherlock Holmes, Consulting Detective...Strategy Guide
Sid Meier's Civilization, or Rome on 640K a Day
Sid Meier's Civilization II: The Official Strategy Guide
Sid Meier's Colonization: The Official Strategy Guide
SimCity 2000: Power, Politics, and Planning
SimEarth: The Official Strategy Guide
SimFarm Almanac: The Official Guide to SimFarm
SimIsle: The Official Strategy Guide
SimLife: The Official Strategy Guide
SimTower: The Official Strategy Guide
SSN-21 Seawolf: The Official Strategy Guide
Star Crusader: The Official Strategy Guide
Stonekeep: The Official Strategy Guide
Strike Commander: The Official Strategy Guide
Stunt Island: The Official Strategy Guide
SubWar 2050: The Official Strategy Guide
Thunderscape: The Official Strategy Guide
TIE Fighter: Defender of the Empire—The Official Strategy Guide
TIE Fighter Collector's CD-ROM: The Official Strategy Guide
Under a Killing Moon: The Official Strategy Guide
WarCraft: Orcs & Humans Official Secrets & Solutions
WarCraft II: Tides of Darkness—The Official Strategy Guide
Warlords II Deluxe: The Official Strategy Guide
Werewolf Vs. Commanche: The Official Strategy Guide
Wing Commander I, II, and III: The Ultimate Strategy Guide
X-COM Terror From The Deep: The Official Strategy Guide
X-COM UFO Defense: The Official Strategy Guide
X-Wing Collector's CD-ROM: The Official Strategy Guide

How to Order:

For information on quantity discounts contact the publisher: Prima Publishing, P.O. Box 1260BK, Rocklin, CA 95677-1260; (916) 632-4400. On your letterhead include information concerning the intended use of the books and the number of books you wish to purchase. For individual orders, turn to the back of the book for more information.

Visit us online at http://www.primapublishing.com

DIABLO™

THE OFFICIAL STRATEGY GUIDE

JOHN WATERS

PRIMA PUBLISHING
Rocklin, California
(916) 632-4400

Project Editor: Chris Balmain

ISBN: 7615-2896-2
Library of Congress Catalog Card Number: 9   72243
Printed in the United States of America

00 01 02 03 DD 10 9 8 7 6 5 4 3 2 1

Contents

I

Introduction

Y ou find yourself in a somber, twilit village. Something evil haunts this place, though the nature of that evil is not immediately clear. An anxious and dwinding populace speaks to you of invasion by dark riders, and of strange rituals performed in a ruined cathedral at the edge of town.

At the entrance to the church, a dying man writhes in agony. Dim light seeps from the church doorway. Within, a stone stairway plunges down into darkness, to a dungeon where the scent of death surrounds you . . .

The labyrinth is no place for the faint of heart—or weak of stomach.

Thus begins *Diablo*, Blizzard's genre-busting, real time role-playing juggernaut. This is a huge game, packed with monsters and mayhem.

The action takes place on 16 dungeon levels, which also house a random mix of peripheral environments. As the hero of the *Diablo* Saga, players must win, buy, or barter for a staggering array of armaments and magic spells, and learn to use them properly against an equally impressive list of foes. Along the way, challenging quests, fascinating plot elements, and a variety of intriguing nonplayer characters will test your gaming mettle.

In short, *Diablo*'s dark database is *massive*.

Few computer games on the market offer a similar range of options. Levels, weapons, monsters—just about everything in this game generates randomly. Each time you fire it up, the map changes, the cast of characters shuffles, and the possibilities shift. Play the Rogue, and it's one game; play the Warrior, it's another; sally forth as the Sorcerer, and it's another game, still. And, once you've beaten the living hell out of your computer, you can play it over the Net with friends (or enemies) in a multiplayer format that expands the game even further, allowing you to crank up the difficulty to suit your skills.

Providing a strategy guide to such a richly constructed and unpredictable game was a tricky—and absolutely essential—venture.

There's so much you can miss, so many possible twists, turns, and subtle aspects you might never notice in the heat of real-time combat . . . so damned many ways to *die* . . .

Without some kind of resource outside the confines of the game, many players would fail to experience everything this grievous adventure has to offer. And that would be a shame.

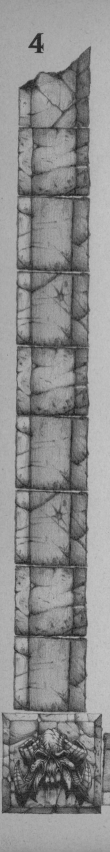

In your hands is the closest thing available to a definitive guide of a random world. It was assembled with the cooperation of the developers, as well as an army of weary-but-devoted testers, and includes every trick and tactic that could be wheedled, cajoled, and begged from the folks at Blizzard.

With this book to accentuate your own skill and determination, the demon Diablo doesn't stand a chance in hell. . . .

2

HOW TO USE THIS BOOK

To a certain breed of role-player, this book's very existence is an insult; a "cheat." Others will see this guide as a welcome torch in a long, dark tunnel. Both points of view are justified. There's nothing quite like an uncompromising win—but there's also no point in sacrificing your sanity to the game gods. Even if you don't want help with specific quests, this book is still worth a read for the deeper understanding of the game's subtleties. If, on the other hand, you find yourself repeating the same mistakes, you probably need a little assist, and you've come to the right place.

Danger lurks around every corner.

Diablo: The Official Strategy Guide is a ready reference to improve your understanding of the game. It includes an overview, information about the interface and heroes, and specific definitions for everything—from character stats to items that may pop from a dying Demon's grasp or shattered barrel. It also includes complete lists of monsters, weapons, and spells.

Players who want straight answers will find lots of them in Chapter 8 (the summary of each quest). If you find yourself at Diablo's door for the 12th time, and *still* can't finish him off, therein lie the strategies you need. Chapter 9 covers multiplayer tactics for Blizzard's

Death becomes a familiar sight.

Battle.net, a totally different approach to the game. (Chapter 10 introduces the game's creators and takes a behind-the-scenes look at how *Diablo* developed.)

Because of *Diablo*'s randomness, no guide, however thorough, can offer fail-safe solutions. This book may be a torch, but it's no floodlight. It doesn't contain the single best route through the game, because, as Blizzard will attest, none exists.

The information in this book is assembled so that you can find what you need without stumbling over things you've already experienced. It's worth noting that the complete list of quests is never available in any one game. If you find yourself unable to trigger a certain expedition, the reason is that the list was predetermined for that game when you first began, and some quests exclude others.

3

GAME OVERVIEW

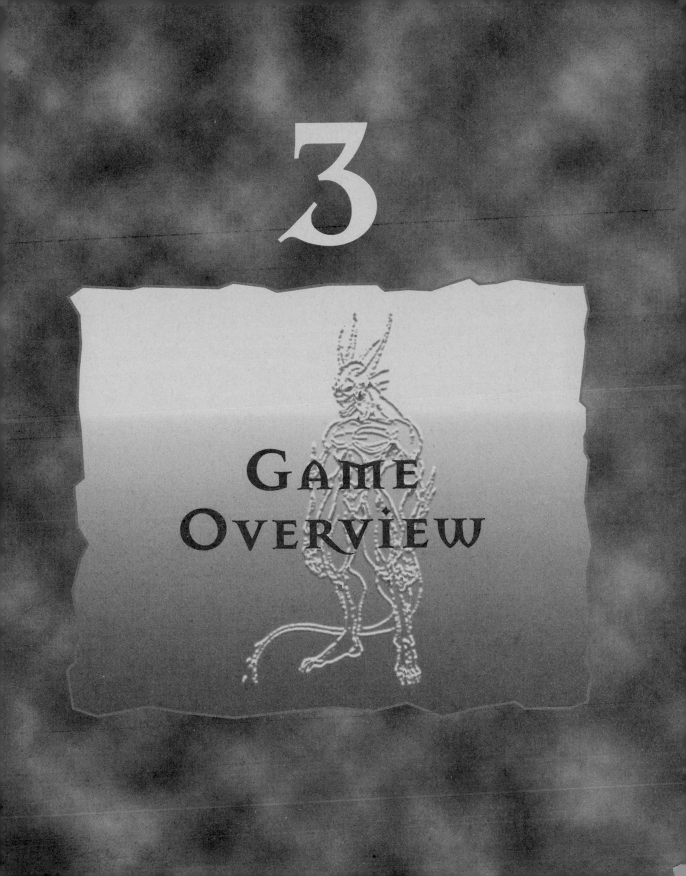

Diablo is an extremely challenging game: You must guide one of three distinct characters through a series of labyrinthine dungeons and cavernous grottos carved deep in the earth near the medieval village of Tristram.

At each level of this subterranean maze, you confront an amazing array of demons, beasts, and undead fiends, all bent on your untimely demise. As you descend, you encounter new creatures of increasing viciousness and power . . . battling for increasingly valuable treasures.

In addition to the treasures you acquire, you'll bolster your various characteristics (strength, dexterity, and so on) as you gain experience in combat. Each increase in experience level rewards you with five points you can distribute amongst the various characteristic categories.

WELCOME TO TRISTRAM

Though the dungeons and caves you explore beneath the earth generate randomly, Tristram's geography remains constant. It's where you begin the game, and it's as good a place as any to begin this discussion of your adventure.

Tristram's inhabitants all have something valuable to say, and these townsfolk trigger the majority of your quests. In addition, some of the citizens have unique abilities you'll take advantage of throughout the game.

CAIN, THE TOWN ELDER

Standing near the town's central fountain, Cain can advise you about the hidden capabilities of any unidentified magical item you might pick up in the dungeon. *Always* identify an item before selling it to ensure that payment corresponds fully to its attributes.

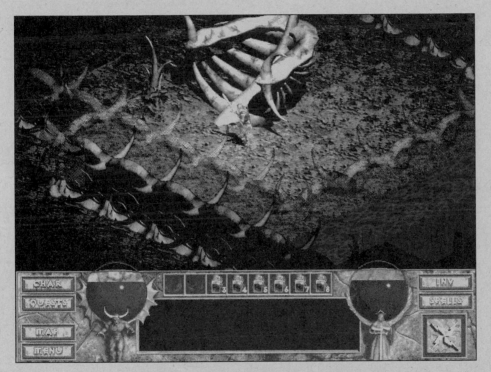

*The cursed cathedral will take you down
to the first level of the labyrinth.*

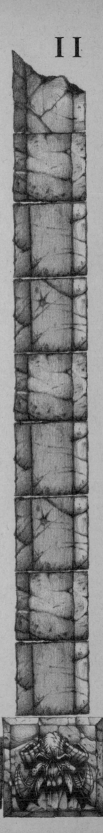

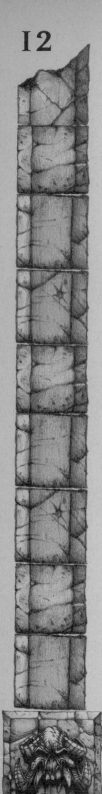

*Cain has a lot to tell anyone patient
enough to stop and listen.*

GRISWOLD, THE BLACKSMITH

Griswold keeps a store of intriguing (and often expensive) weapons and armor at his shop. The list generates randomly, with new items added whenever you make a purchase or advance an experience level. The Blacksmith also has the ability to repair items whose Durability ain't what it used to be, and that's probably when he'll serve you best. Common items can be repaired for next-to-nothing, while magical items require much more expense.

Griswold's services are indispensable.

ADRIA, THE WITCH

Across the stream southeast of town is the hut of Adria the Witch, the only place you can purchase Mana potions. Additionally, the witch offers a constant and diverse supply of magical items for sale, including potions, scrolls, books, and staffs. And, at a very reasonable price, she'll recharge any magic staffs. If you're playing the Sorcerer, you'll always want to check the Witch's supply before making other expenditures, just in case she has a rare and valuable Spellbook or Scroll you might need—they don't sell cheap.

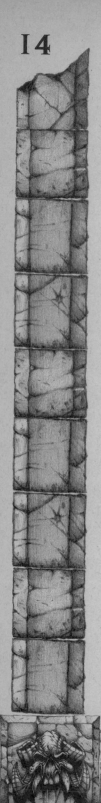

Adria is the one to see when the subject is Magic.

Whatever class you're playing, you'll want to take advantage of the Witch's supply of Town Portal and Identify scrolls. The Identify scrolls cost the same as getting the service from Cain, allowing you to utilize magical gear found in the dungeon without taking it back to Tristram first. By the same token, the Town Portal spell is an indispensible means of returning to town without putting in a lot of tedious leg-work.

PEPIN, THE HEALER

As you might expect, Pepin heals. Just as the witch supplies Mana, Pepin peddles potions and scrolls for healing, with miscellaneous elixirs thrown in late in the game for variety. He'll also bring you back to full health for no charge, and in the multiplayer games you'll find that Pepin carries a steady supply of Ressurect scrolls.

Pepin can heal what ails you.

WIRT, THE PEG-LEGGED BOY

Gnawed on by monsters, Wirt escaped the dungeon with his life, though you'll often wonder if that was such a good thing. For 50 gold pieces, Wirt will divulge his current item (singular) for sale, and it's usually worth the price to take a peek. Wirt whispers for your attention across the stream behind Gillian's house, in a small clearing beneath a tree. Just as with Griswold's list of Premium items, Wirt features a new treasure at random intervals.

TIP

IF WIRT HAS A RELATIVELY CHEAP ITEM FOR SALE, SUCH AS A SCROLL, IT MIGHT BE WORTH BUYING IT EVEN IF YOU DON'T NEED IT, JUST TO COAX HIM INTO RE-STOCKING.

Wirt is nobody's friend, but he might have just the weapon you need.

OGDEN, GILLIAN, AND FARNHAM

Tristram's bit players include the Tavern Owner, Barmaid, and Town Drunk. Though they'll occasionally begin a quest or divulge some semi-useful information, they generally fill in details of stories that other citizens initiate.

*Gillian is beloved in Tristram, but her role
in Diablo is that of a bit player.*

QUESTING

Once you're acquainted with the townsfolk, it's time to explore the labyrinth beneath the church. You'll find that the good people of Tristram often have some task they'd like you to perform while the monsters are nipping at your heels. Most quests consist of snatching something from the dungeon, and then trading it in town for other items or services.

You can ignore the townsfolk's requests, but it's frequently bet-

Farnham's story is a sad one, when it's coherent at all.

ter to honor them. Hey, you're down in the dungeon anyway; if the Witch wants to get her hands on a Black Mushroom, you might as well bring it back. You need all the friends you can get . . . .

Realize that there are some quests which always appear in the game, while others are selected from specific sets. These quests are chosen randomly as each game begins. Though certain actions may trigger certain scenarios, you cannot trigger any quest you want. For their complete listing, their groupings, and some tactical advice, check the "Quests" chapter.

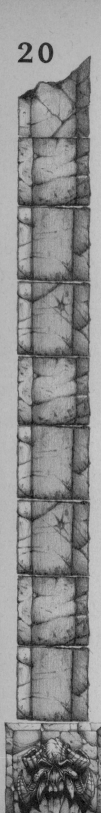

GENERAL EXPLORATION

Slow and careful is the best way to approach exploring the caverns beneath Tristram's church. Sure, you can stride from room to room brashly, hoping simply to swat aside any opposition. Inevitably, though, this approach will land you smack in the middle of more monsters than you'll find in a Steven King novel.

Always save your game before accessing a Shrine, the better to consider its effects before committing to them.

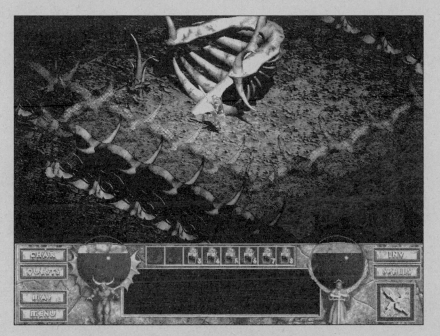

Stay sharp; stay alive.

In a matter of speaking, exploration is a combat-related topic, and that's discussed in more depth later on. Just keep in mind, however, that you'll want to tackle each dungeon one room at a time, rarely bypassing anything, and certainly never running head-long into an unexplored area with pursuers hot on your heels.

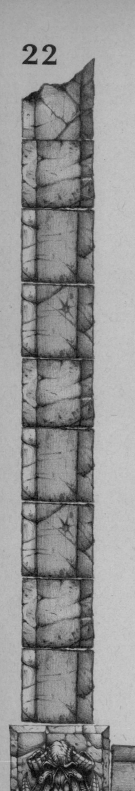

TIP

GETTING BACK TO TRISTRAM FROM THE
DUNGEON IS USUALLY STRAIGHTFORWARD, AS
DIRECT AVENUES EXIST EVEN FROM DEEP
UNDERGROUND. THERE'S NO GOOD REASON TO

*The libraries are often well-guarded, but the books
they hold are always worth the fight.*

OVEREXTEND YOURSELF WHEN YOU CAN ALWAYS MAKE A QUICK TRIP TOPSIDE TO REPLENISH HEALTH AND MANA. IN ADDITION TO THE MAIN DUNGEON ENTRANCE THROUGH THE FRONT DOOR OF THE CATHEDRAL, THERE ARE STAIRWAYS DEEP IN THE DUNGEON THAT OPEN AVENUES LEADING TO TRISTRAM. ON THE FIFTH LEVEL, THE STAIRS EMERGE FROM THE CRYPT IN THE GRAVEYARD. ON THE NINTH LEVEL, THE STAIRS TO TOWN LEAD TO A CAVE NEAR WHERE WIRT STANDS. FINALLY, ON LEVEL 13, TAKING THE UP STAIRCASE OPENS A FISSURE IN THE GROUND BEHIND PEPIN'S HOUSE, THROUGH WHICH YOU CAN RETURN TO HELL.

SHORT OF TAKING THE STAIRS, THE TOWN PORTAL SPELL IS THE QUICKEST ROUTE. IT OPENS A DIRECT GATEWAY TO A SPOT JUST OUTSIDE TRISTRAM'S TOWN SQUARE. THE SPELL IS A TWO-WAY TRIP, ALLOWING YOU TO ACCESS THE TOWN, AND THEN RETURN TO THE DUNGEON FROM THE EXACT POINT WHERE YOU CAST THE SPELL. ADRIA THE WITCH KEEPS A STEADY SUPPLY OF TOWN PORTAL SPELLS. CONSIDER THAT YOU DON'T NEED TO BE CARRYING FIVE OR SIX WITH YOU AT ALL TIMES: IF YOU FIND MORE THAN ONE IN THE DUNGEON, THROW THE EXTRAS ON THE GROUND NEAR WHERE THE PORTAL OPENS IN TRISTRAM, AND PICK ONE UP WHEN YOU RETURN TO TOWN.

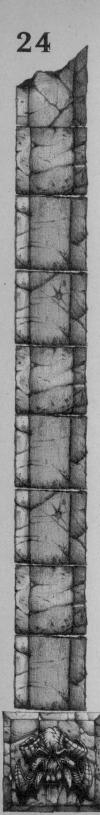

When you reach the catacombs, the mausoleum will open so you can return to the town from that level.

THE INTERFACE

Diablo's manual dissects the controlling interface nicely, but the following practical considerations can further enhance your enjoyment of the game. Once you get used to the various menus at hand, configuring and moving your character efficiently becomes second nature. This will leave you free to concentrate vanquishing the masters of darkness.

The boxes, barrels, and sarcophagi can hold treasures, weapons, magic—and pain.

PROPER CONFIGURATION

At the start of the adventure, you have precious few weapons and armor, so configuration isn't critical. As you begin knocking treasure loose from dungeon denizens, however, and you accumulate enough gold to purchase upgrades, configuring your character properly separates the breathing heroes from the dead.

You'll soon note *Diablo*'s huge list of items and magical characteristics. Each item can take on a myriad of magical aspects.

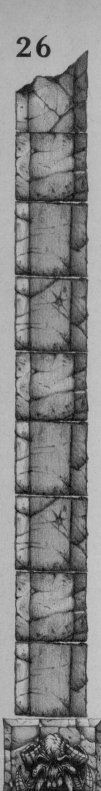

The Character Information Screen lets you keep track of the essential statistics of the character you're building.

Determining those best-suited to your character would be tedious if you attempted to do so based purely on data analysis.

Placing Character and Inventory screens side by side as you equip two items lets you view the results as the pertinent numbers change on the Character menu. Often, you'll end up sacrificing something in one column to gain a significant advantage in another.

In the purest sense, you'll ready your hero for either close or distance combat, with magical or nonmagical components. As you progress, you'll find rings or amulets that magically enhance certain characteristics, or likewise offer your character specific defensive advantages. It's these items you'll most often equip and remove throughout the game, as you pump up specific character traits for impending confrontations.

As with choosing weapons, when you call up Character and Inventory, think about what you're likely to encounter in the dungeon ahead, and emphasize the appropriate abilities. This is more of a crapshoot as you begin each dungeon level, because you never know what lies ahead. After a few rooms, however, you get a feel

When you reach the caves, another entrance
to the surface will open.

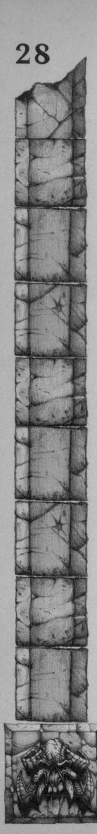

for the level's monster populace, and the kind of combat likely in store. Stop and equip with the most common monsters in mind, then prepare a second configuration to handle the other denizens.

TAKING INVENTORY

The space in your inventory is limited, so don't carry around a lot of junk.

As you collect treasure, you'll constantly face the dilemma of what to equip, what to carry with you, and what to leave on the dungeon floor.

Hang onto all magical items, especially early in the game. You'll know an item has magical properties by the blue text description that comes up when you discover the item lying on the floor, and also by the "Not Identified" designation you can see after the item is added to your inventory.

Even if *you* can't use or don't particularly want some item of treasure, you can unload anything you find for quick cash up in Tristram, through either the Blacksmith or the Witch. Getting those goodies back to town can be a logistical problem, however. So can discovering a valuable, but as yet unusable, piece of equipment, scroll, or book. Keep the following in mind for just such quandaries.

NOW OR LATER?

When you're traveling through the dungeon, rich with Health and Mana, it would be foolish to drop your quest and hike back to town to sell your spoils. Let your Health and Mana levels dictate when

*When you reach the hell levels, another
way to the town level will appear.*

you return to Tristram, unless the floor is becoming so littered with treasure that you're afraid you're going to lose track of it all. And be selective about what you take back to town.

Obviously, you should take back all magical items for identification before considering whether to sell them. Also, bring back any duplicate items (if you find an axe and you already have one, for instance) if there's any doubt as to which is the better piece of equipment. Let Griswold's offering price be your guide.

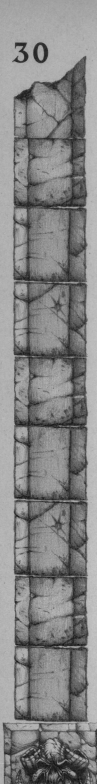

But how do you carry all that equipment and still hang onto the stuff you're positive you want to keep?

You don't.

Take only the things that you want to sell. Leave everything else in a pile on the dungeon floor, near your portal or the stairway to town. Nothing will disappear while you're gone, and you greatly increase the amount of goodies you can take back to Tristram. Equip weapons and wear armor you intend to unload to further increase your carrying capacity, then re-outfit when you return to the labyrinth.

Likewise, if you find an excellent weapon, book, or scroll you can't use yet, but want to hang onto, don't waste valuable inventory space dragging it around the dungeon. Take it to Tristram, and throw it on the ground. It won't go anywhere. As your specific abilities increase, reclaim the relevant item. (Note: If you start a *new* game with the same character, any objects left on the ground *will* disappear.)

Primary Character Traits

As you slash your way toward Diablo, your fledgling adventurer will gain Experience. At each successive Experience level you receive five points to distribute among your hero's various traits. Character traits are discussed in greater detail in Chapter 4; however, keep the following in mind as you dole out those five precious points.

First, it may be unwise to let one area fall disproportionately far behind the others. Each primary category directly affects crucial components that can make your character a more formidable and more durable adventurer. You'll certainly want to build the character trait that your class is most dependent upon, but every area is important to a well-rounded adventurer: Good weapons and armor require Strength. Good spells require high Magic knowledge. A devastating bow attack needs serious Dexterity. And all the classes need Vitality: The stuff of life.

Vitality for the Warrior means you'll be awarded two more Hit Points to your total. Though it isn't very exciting, you should probably put one of those precious five points per level into Vitality. The same goes for the Sorcerer and Magic. Every point into Magic increases a Sorcerers Mana by two.

Though the various character traits have some obvious and direct effects, there are also subtle adjustments made as you increase the various totals. Consider the following:

- *Strength* dictates the weapons you can wield, as well as the damage you inflict.
- *Magic Points* (MPs) determine not only the spells you can learn, but their effectiveness and the economy with which you expend Mana. Increasing MPs increases your Mana capacity correspondingly.
- *Dexterity* influences not only proficiency with ranged weapons, but also a character's accuracy in close combat, armor class, and movement rate.
- *Vitality* directly affects your character's Health capacity, increasing the damage you can withstand from a single blow. When you start to fight monsters that can deal out tremendous damage, you want to be able to live through at least a single hit.

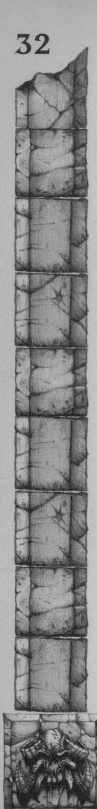

OTHER CHARACTERISTICS

Your character's primary attributes, as you'll notice when points are distributed and magical enhancements become more common, influence other character traits in ways both dramatic and slight. If you've played a *Dungeons & Dragons*–type game before, the concept will be familiar, though specific calculations are, of course, unique to *Diablo*.

A drink from the Blood Fountain restores your character's Health.

ARMOR CLASS

The *Armor Class* number measures how well-protected your character is from physical harm. It sums up the Armor Class ratings of everything he or she is wearing, including any magical enhancements (or penalties). The higher the Armor Class number, the better.

TO HIT PERCENTAGE

The To Hit percentage measures your character's chances of hitting an average opponent in combat. This number only reflects your

The tomes tell the tail of the Dark Exile.

character's chance To Hit, without considering the specific opponent in question: Your To Hit number is a baseline, used in calculating your chance of hitting a specific monster in combat by subratacting the monster's Armor Class and then taking a various number of other factors into consideration. Practically speaking, take your To Hit number and subratact your target's Armor Class to see if you're in the ball park.

DAMAGE

The Damage number is the range of Hit Points you'll damage a monster each time you land a blow. Again, this is a baseline number; actual Damage results from a calculation that incorporates your attack abilities plus the specific monster's defenses.

RESIST MAGIC

This number measures your character's resistance to Magic-based attacks. Early in the game, this is rarely a factor, since fire and lightning are more common than this type of Magic near the top of the dungeon. Once you begin to battle Succubi, this becomes a much more important factor. In the bottom of the dungeon, your ability to shrug off hostile Magic often can mean the difference between life and death.

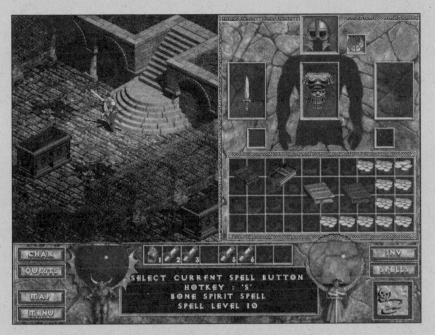

*The Inventory Screen shows you what your
character is wearing and carrying*

Resist Fire

Probably the most common magical attack is a fire-based spell, so
allocate points to this number before venturing too deeply. Watch
for fire-resistant weapons or armor. It's often worth hanging onto a
lesser piece of equipment just for the magical protection. Magical
attacks don't consider Armor Class or have any effect on an item's
Durability, so even some Rags might be worth leaving up in Tristram if they feature a high enough fire resistance.

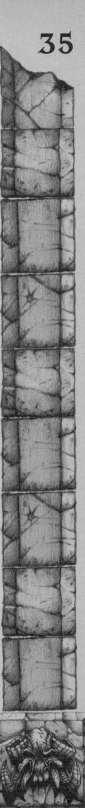

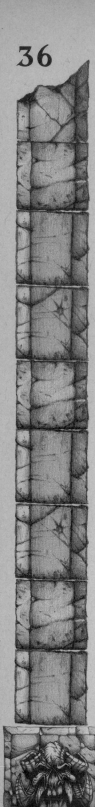

Resist Lightning

If someone's firing magical bolts at you, and it looks like *lightning*, that's because it is. That's a generalization, but electrical attacks become increasingly more common as you make your descent.

Other Features, Random Insights

Beyond the specifics of equipping your character, understanding a couple of interface nuances up front will help make your *Diablo* experience more entertaining.

Hey! I Said Time Out!

Diablo's action never stops (short of calling up the menu screen, which prevents manipulating the game in any way). The saga continues even when Character and Inventory screens block the dungeon view. Opening only one of these menus will give you a slightly eclipsed view of the action. That's an effective way to make hasty adjustments during full retreat. If you plan on tinkering, save the game first. Monsters won't be merciful just because you're fishing around in your backpack. The Pause hotkey ('P') serves the same purpose as the menu, but the menu serves as a better 'panic button.' From the menu, you can reload your last saved game.

The Quest Log lets you refresh your memory.

THE AUTOMAP

One of the nicest features in the game just happens to be the Automap, which gives a top-down view of the dungeon, filling in areas as you explore. And the best trick to know about the Automap is that you can scroll the map without moving your character by utilizing the arrow keys on the keyboard. It's fairly essential, and certainly prudent, to clear an entire level of dungeon before venturing to the next. Be sure to review the map to make sure there are no blank areas before you proceed.

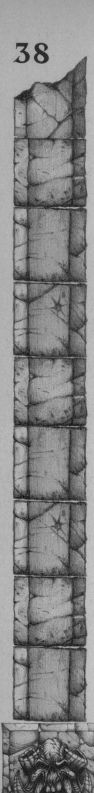

TIP

WATCH FOR A SHRINE IN THE GAME WHICH
REPORTS "THE WAY IS MADE CLEAR WHEN
VIEWED FROM ABOVE." YOU GUESSED IT: THE
AUTOMAP IS SUDDENLY COMPLETE, REGARDLESS
OF WHERE YOU'VE BEEN ON THE LEVEL. WHILE IT
CAN BE HELPFUL, THIS IS NOT A GOOD THING IF
YOU'RE USING THE MAP TO CHECK FOR CLEARED
AREAS, AND ONE MORE REASON YOU SHOULD
ALWAYS SAVE THE GAME BEFORE ACCESSING A
SHRINE, JUST IN CASE.

SPELL LEVELS

Reading two of the same type of Spellbook increases your level of
expertise with that spell. The spell costs less Mana to perform, does
greater damage to an enemy, and lasts longer with each level it
climbs.

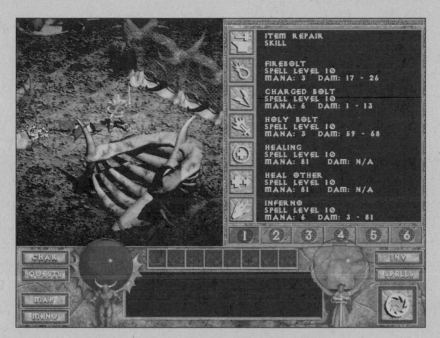

*The Spellbook gives a detailed account
of your inventory of magic.*

SPELL HOTKEYS

Spell hotkeys allow you to throw more than one spell without calling up the onscreen Spellbook. Once you've learned a couple of spells, it's a good idea to establish some. If your playing the Sorcerer, where a quick and efficient combat sequence is essential to your survival, the hotkeys can be a real life-saver. To assign a hotkey, click on the large current spell square, and similar squares for all the spells appear across the screen. Next, position the cursor

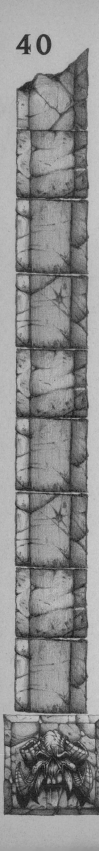

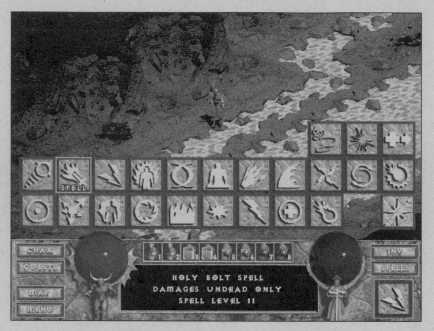

Use the Spellbook for quick spell access.

over the spell (or skill icon) of your choice, and press the F5–F8 keys to assign the spell. Just as you would configure your armor and weapons for specific combat situations, you should constantly be juggling your hotkey lineup to suit the immediate opponent. When you're not sure about a monster's immunities, hotkey both a Fire- and a Lightning-based spell, and test 'em out on the crowd.

COLOR CODES

In *Diablo*, the color of an icon, a caption, and even an object can tell you a lot about that item's nature. Become familiar with the following color identifiers.

SPEEDBOOK

- Gold = Skill. This is an inherent characteristic of your character, which improves with skill level
- Blue = Learned Spell. Once you learn a spell, it's yours for the duration of the game, under most circumstances.
- Red = Scroll. A scroll has one use only. Once you exhaust a particular scroll, it disappears from your inventory.
- Orange = Staff. A staff, which you use as a weapon, has a limited power supply, but you may recharge it under certain circumstances.

ITEM DESCRIPTIONS

- White = Normal
- Blue = Magic
- Gold = Unique

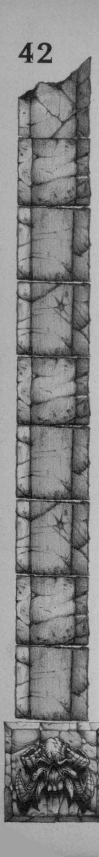

GENERAL MOVEMENT

Navigating *Diablo*'s world quickly and efficiently is a fundamental skill, but, as with many of the game's aspects, mastering the subtleties can make you more of a force to be reckoned with.

Notice that when you move in large, clear areas—especially the town—placing the cursor near the edge of the screen and holding down the left mouse button lets you travel in that direction, scrolling the screen as you go.

When moving in the dungeon, however, keep the cursor within an inch-and-a-half of your hero, or you'll constantly be strolling into hordes of monsters. By moving forward in small increments, you can often draw out the monsters a few at a time, as opposed to rousting the entire populace of a large area with one careless pass.

4

THE CHARACTERS

D*iablo* gives you a choice between three uniquely talented hero archetypes familiar to role-players for decades—the Warrior, the Rogue, and the Sorcerer.

The Warrior is strong and vigorous, the Rogue agile and clever, and the Sorcerer especially gifted in the magical arts. Any class can develop the strengths of the others, although not to the same extent. Thus, picking a character for *Diablo* is a matter of personal preference, and examining each character beforehand will keep you from making a selection that conflicts with your style of play.

Regardless of the class you select, it's always good to have a "Plan B." One-trick ponies don't get very far in *Diablo*, so don't dump all your Experience Points into a couple of traits. By the same token, don't sit on the fence. Pretend your character has a split personality—a primary and a secondary configuration, if you will.

Sorcerey is the 'pivot point' of *Diablo* in regard to a character's abilities. That is: A Sorcerer can choose to emulate either a Warrior or a Rogue, in a manner of speaking. But the Warrior and Rogue classes are so similar, in purest combat terms (i.e. they're non-magical) that it really behooves both to cultivate a magical attack for battling foes that simply can't be dealt with effectively otherwise.

Ultimately, you'll find that each of the character classes has an inherent ability that dictates its most effective fighting style. That unique aspect of each class further adds to the dynamic nature of *Diablo*, and greatly heightens the game's replayability. Don't short-change yourself by never experimenting outside the Warrior class, or you'll be missing two-thirds of the fun.

THE WARRIOR

The strongest and toughest class, the Warrior, excels in hand-to-hand combat. His natural strength, properly cultivated, allows him to utilize heavy armor, cumbrous axes, weighty clubs, and massive blades that are beyond the means of most Sorcerers and Rogues.

The Warrior is also a skillful craftsman, possessing an inherent ability to repair weapons and armor in the field (although he's no match for a true blacksmith). As with all the charcter classes, the Warrior's aptitude with his special skill increases with each level of experience earned (see next tip).

Though Griswold can repair any item up to its current available Durability, the price runs high when magical or Unique items are involved. Unless an item is so obviously irreplacable that you never want to lower its Durability, it makes sense to have the Warrior effect repairs as opposed to paying for them.

In the middle of the game, when various suits of armor and weapons become available, the Warrior's skill is most valuable. Though an item eventually 'wears down' after repeated repair jobs from the Warrior, you'll invariably pick up something as a replacement before things begin to get knocked from your body in battle.

The Warrior comes into his prime midway through the game, when a large axe and an attitude is all it takes to deal effectively with the general population. At the beginning of the game, expect to use down plenty of Health Scrolls and Potions as you grapple at close quarters. Late in the game, be sure to have your three magical resistances pumped up, or the bottom-dwellers of the dungeon will have their way with you from afar.

As eluded to in the chapter introduction, the last word on the Warrior, oddly enough, is Sorcery. Though it also pays to be proficient with a bow, the Warrior is the one character class capable of running right up and bashing on someone to do physical damage, and it's a little silly to take that away from him. There's also the consideration of the increased Armor Class that comes with a shield, which a bow prevents a Warrior from enjoying.

When you're not putting experience points in Strength and Vitality, drop a couple into Magic. Late in the game, when everyone has a Magic attack, you won't feel so outgunned. Though you'll never have the Spellbook of a true Sorcerer, yours will be plenty strong enough. Keep your eye out for the books of Stone Curse, Chain Lightning, Inferno, Teleport, and/or Flame Wave. Those'll be the upper end of what you can hope to utilize as a Warrior, and indeed they'll serve you

TIP

A CHARACTER'S SPECIAL SKILL

EACH OF THE THREE CLASSES OF CHARACTER COMES EQUIPPED WITH ITS OWN SPECIAL SKILL: AN INNATE ABILITY THAT HELPS IT NAVIGATE THE dungeon a little more effectively than the other classes in one regard.

For the Warrior, that skill is repairing worn items, as measured by the items Durability number.

The Sorcerer posseses the ability to recharge staves, an ability analogous to the Warrior's.

The Rogue has a certain skill at identifying disarming traps, specifically booby-trapped chests and doors.

In short, if you're playing the Warrior or Sorcerer, wait as long as you can to repair or recharge, realizing that, in the case of the Warrior, an item vanishes when its Durability number reaches zero. The longer you wait, the more experience your character will have gained, and they'll do a significantly better job, as reflected by the lowering of the upper-end Durability or Charges number.

If you're playing the Rogue, a trapped chest will show up as such on the menu when you highlight it. Select your disarming skill as you would a spell, and 'cast' it on the offending object.

well. Also be on the lookout for weapons or armor that carry a Magic component, either adding to your own Strength or bolstering resistances. That's an easy way to kill two birds with one stone.

Warrior Maximum Ability Totals

Strength	250
Magic	50
Dexterity	60
Vitality	100

The Warrior is the master of hand-to-hand combat.

Why Play the Warrior

Blizzard's resident Diablo ace, Roman Kenney, shares his best tips on the Warrior.

- The Warrior enjoys the fastest attacks with all weapons except the bow.
- He gains two Hit Points per level of experience, and also per point of Vitality.
- The Warrior's Repair Skill makes him low-maintenance.
- He gets double bonuses for all items 'of Life' and 'of Vitality,' though he also gets double negatives.
- The Warrior has a Critical Strike component giving him a calculated chance for double damage (half of his current level is his chance— e.g. A level 10 Warrior has a 5% chance for Critical Strike).
- His high Vitality means he takes less damage per hit.

A Warrior's Insights

- The Stone Curse spell is the most effective way to keep enemies from running away.
- The Teleport spell effectively closes gaps with distant attackers.
- Flash is a good crowd-control spell, and relatively Mana-economical.
- Keep something in your inventory to augment magical abilities, thus allowing you to cast the high-end spells.
- Use potions or scrolls for healing, not the spell.

The Rogue

The Rogue character, long the abandoned wasteland of role-playing games, stakes out new territory in *Diablo*. Until you've hoisted the bow, you'll never suspect the truly devastating impact it can have when properly wielded, and the Rogue has the potential to fully exploit its merciless nature.

Especially in the early levels of the dungeon, while the Warrior is using Health at an expensive rate and the Sorcerer is likewise going through Mana, the Rogue stands back at a distance, or peeks through gratings, building experience levels rapidly at the expense of the lesser monsters.

One of the mysterious Sisters of the Sightless Eye, the Rogue's "sixth sense" allows her to perceive and disarm traps before they spring. She should keep her distance from the more powerful monsters until she's bolstered her Vitality and found some decent armor.

As with the Warrior, the Rogue should work to cultivate strong magical components to attack and defense, though the Rogue may want to use Magic almost in lieu of hand-to-hand combat: She already has a ranged attack. With the armor restrictions placed on the class by its lesser Strength, it's good to be able to throw the proverbial "kitchen sink" at an enemy if and when it manages to appear right beside you.

First and foremost, of course, the Rogue should endeavor to be a devastating bowman . . . bow*woman* . . . at the expense of everything else. Crank up the Dexterity, and save your gold. If you can't knock loose a decent bow from the dungeon, buy one as soon as the opportunity presents itself.

The Rogue should, for all practical intents and purposes, never enter a battle without a bow in hand. Armor, in the form of capes and caps, is dirt cheap, and a decent bow can keep all your enemies dying at a distance anyway. For specific insights regarding fighting with the bow, check the chapter on combat. Though enagaging with the bow is markedly different than any other attack form in the game, it's worth the effort to perfect it.

ROGUE MAXIMUM ABILITY TOTALS

Strength	55
Magic	70
Dexterity	250
Vitality	80

The Rogue shines in the area of physical distance attacks.

WHY PLAY THE ROGUE?

Blizzard's own Roman Kenney shares his tactical insights on the Rogue character.

- The Rogue casts spells much faster than the Warrior.
- She adds both one Health and one Mana point per level gained.
- She can inflict physical damage from a distance with a bow.
- She fires the bow very quickly and accurately.

A ROGUE'S INSIGHTS

- With very few exceptions, the Rogue should fight with the bow.
- The Mana Shield spell is almost as important for the Rogue as for the Sorcerer.
- Keep both Heal and Mana Shield hot-keyed.
- Stone Curse and a decent bow are a deadly combination.
- Open doors with Telekinesis and fire arrows through the portal from a distance.

THE SORCERER

The Sorcerer is, of course, the master of magic. A member of the Brotherhood of the Vizjerei, he's especially adept at utilizing scrolls and spells. Right from the start, magic is his natural weapon; his special skill is the ability to recharge staffs, and as he gains experience, the Sorcerer learns spells much more quickly than his counterparts.

The downside to throwing all the coolest spells is, of course, that the monsters take it personally, and they'd really love to get their hands on you for just a second or two . . . occasionally, they do, and so the Sorcerer has to be concerned with defense, especially at the very start of the game. The best defense, later in the game, is often a good offense: Once you start throwing the high-end spells around, namely Stone Curse, Chain Lightning, Flame Wave, and the occasional dose of Elemental, all you have to worry about is buying Mana.

It behooves the Sorcerer to invest in Strength, to allow the use of better armor, and Vitality, to serve as a cushion against those nasty close encounters. Don't go crazy with the Vitality, however: Basically, you need to survive long enough to get your hands on some of those Mana Shield Scrolls from the witch—or better yet, a book of Mana Shield. If you can manage to throw a Mana Shield Spell before every significant chunk of adventuring, you're Magic Points then function as Hit Points. If you've been pouring earned Experience Points into Magic early in the game, it can really pay off later on due to the Mana Shield. From then on, you can just buy potions of Full Mana, utilizing them as both health and magic power. Though you'll burn Mana like crazy, you can, in effect, be replenishing both health and magical power for the price of a full Mana dose, and that's a bargain.

One final note on the Mana Shield: Since it wears off when you employ the Town Portal Spell or travel between levels, and you're generally going to be casting it from a scroll, try not to use it unless you're going to be staying a while at that level. Clean house before you start taking goodies back to Tristam.

SORCERER MAXIMUM ABILITY TOTALS

Strength	45
Magic	250
Dexterity	85
Vitality	80

If you like Mana, you're a Sorcerer.

Why Play the Sorcerer?

Blizzard's Roman Kenney shares some of the mage's primary advantages.

- The Sorcerer gains two points of Mana for every level gained, as well as for every point of Magic.
- He gets double the bonus for magical enhancements (but he also gets double negatives).
- At the higher levels, he's almost indestructible, unless mobbed.
- He attacks fastest with the shield.
- For every level of Mana Shield, the damage he takes is reduced.

A Sorcerer's Insights

- Use Teleport to escape from crowds.
- Always have a Mana Shield spell in effect.
- Pour points into the Magic characteristic, since Mana serves as both magic power and Hit Points with the Mana Shield spell in effect.
- The combination of Golem and Stone Curse is perhaps the only way for a Sorcerer to triumph over Diablo's minions on Hell difficulty: Send your Golem into a room, and watch for him to come under attack. Stone Curse in the area of the magic attack until the magic stops. You don't need a line-of-sight to Stone Curse.

TIP

Don't feel you must distribute newly acquired Experience Points immediately. Sometimes, it's better to wait and see what the dungeon holds in store, and what new treasures await in Tristram. Perhaps you'll discover (or can purchase) a magical item to increase your stats dramatically in one category. Since you'll probably want to go back to town after going up an Experience level, just to see what new items are in the townsfolks' inventories, you might even wait to check out the supplies before distributing points. If the difference in utilizing a coveted new item is one or two Experience Points, you'll be glad you waited as long as it takes to get to Town.

BIT PLAYERS

In addition to your character and the townsfolk of Tristram, several unique creatures in the dungeon appear as part of certain quests, or leading a horde of monsters. These are *Diablo*'s bit players, deserving of mention as such, but not worth discussing individually.

Without exception, these monsters are tests of your abilities, and that's how you should use them. Even if you just barely squeak by a Unique monster, it usually means you're ready for the dungeon beyond. Conversely, if one kicks your butt time and again, you lack something in either your attribute totals or your tactical approach.

Be wary that some Uniques are serious curveballs: They are restant or immune to magic that kills the common variety most effectively. If you devastate a pack of uglies with magic, and the Unique remains relatively unscathed, get the hint and switch to Plan B, or you'll burn up an excessive amount of resources to get the job done. As with other monsters, a Unique should react with some level of distress if the method of attack you're employing is doing a significant amount of damage.

Also realize that, although most Uniques will give chase, they can usually be ditched in the dungeon, allowing you to pilfer anything they might be guarding. You'll probably want to put some distance between you and a Unique, either way, the better to judge its attack strategies and come up with your own. If it's possible to loop around behind the Unique and its horde, and employ a little-hit-and-run, that's usually a very good idea.

In most cases, you'll want to thin out the crowd before dealing with the Unique monster. Otherwise, while you're concentrating your attacks on the hardest monster to kill, six or seven of his minions get to take potshots at you. The cumulative effect of an attacking horde in the time it takes to kill its Unique leader can quite rapidly be deadly. Figure it out.

5

CREATURES AND COMBAT

Beneath Tristram's desecrated cathedral, Diablo's minions wait. Flesh-eating demons, rotting corpses, and winged beasties lurch, swarm, and flutter through the dank rooms and dark halls of this godless abattoir. These Servants of Darkness, 150 types strong, are unique horrors with but one purpose—to kill. Fortunately, armed with knowledge gleaned from this tome, you may yet triumph over this army of evil.

The underworld is dark warriors may be numerous, but fortunately (for the memory-challenged among us) they fall into three more or less familiar (for veteran RPGers) categories—the Undead, Animal-based monsters, and Demons.

These broad categories break down further into templates used to construct the beings that haunt the subterranean lands of Tristram. Thus, the computer selects randomly, or assigns based on game level, from groups of similar monster types.

This chapter will explore combat tactics first, then examine each of the three monster types, and recommend ways to end their pitiful existence. Finally, these types are broken down more specifically, with stats for each monster variation, according to the template that spawned it.

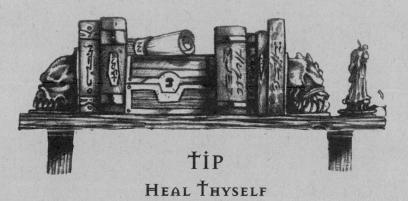

Tip

Heal Thyself

Effectively healing your character in combat is one of the most crucial parts of the game, and there are a couple of nuances that'll go a long way to preserving that healthful glow. The general topic of recovering lost Health and Magic Points is covered on the discusiion concerning Potions in the Magic chapter that follows, but consider that perhaps the best method for healing during combat is the Scroll of Healing. The simple reason is that, unlike potions, scrolls can be hotkeyed. The ability to call up healing in combat with a hotkey, and not burn any Mana to use it, is a huge advantage. Unfortunately, there isn't a limitless supply of Scrolls of Health available. For 50 gold pieces each, you should clean out the inventory of both the Healer and the Witch whenever you visit them. Throw the scrolls on the ground in Tristram if you have enough already: You'll need them eventually, and in ever-increasing numbers.

THE BASICS OF COMBAT

For each of the three distinct character classes in *Diablo*, there exists a markedly different fighting style. Though those differences are evident early on in the game, a little belaboring of the obvious might help prevent a lot of tedious trial and error work.

THE WARRIOR

A brawler. Most of your fighting is going to be done at close quarters, so armor is as important as weapons, as is the ability to deal out big chunks of damage.

When equipping the Warrior, strive to acquire items that provide boosts to Strength, and also feature magic resistance.

Early in the game, you'll want a shield for protection, though midway you can consider switching to a large axe: the ability to kill an opponent quickly can offset the slightly increased frequency of suffering damage-inflicting attacks. Late in the game, you'll probably want to pick up a shield again. The monsters at the bottom of hell can't be killed with a single axe chop, so it becomes more important to protect yourself than to have the difference in damage that you realize between a sword and an axe. Keep in mind though, that a magic axe with a fast hit or fast recovery component makes a lethal combination.

THE ROGUE

The bow is the chosen and preferred weapon of the Rogue. She should literally never have anything else in her hands when going into combat.

Early in the game, do whatever it takes to get a decent bow. Sell everything you own if a bow is available that you can use and even just barely afford. Don't forget to put Experience Points into Strength, so that you'll be able to use larger bows as they become available. For specific tips on employing the bow, see the following section on Ranged Attacks.

From the standpoint of magical enhancements, think about increasing Strength and Vitality, as well as Dexterity. Heavy on the Dexterity. You need an insanely high To Hit percentage to effectively thin out hordes of monsters as you get into the Cavern levels of the dungeon.

When dealing with large hordes of monsters, you actually want to close the gap a little at first. You don't want to charge a single monster, of course, or risk alerting any of its brethren that might be lurking out of view. But unless the area behind you, relatively speaking, has already been cleared, you're going to run into trouble if you fall back. And, almost invariably, you will want to fall back. The advantage of being a bow-slinger is fighting from a distance.

THE SORCERER

As you might suspect, the Sorcerer should devote almost every possible resource to learning spells, and augmenting magical abilities. Strength is also an important factor, since eventually you're going to want some decent armor. You might also consider employing a bow as a means of inflicting physical harm, and in that case you'll want to be just strong enough to wear a suit of armor, and then pour any points not headed for Magic almost exclusively into Dexterity. Unlike the other classes, Vitality is only a concern for the Sorcerer early in the game—due to the Mana Shield.

Buy the Mana Shield Scroll whenever it appears in the Witch's inventory, and count your lucky stars should you lay hands on a book of Mana Shield. With that spell, your Magic Points can be effectively used as a substitute for Hit Points, and that's a very good thing when you're Hit Points are around 80 and your Magic Points are more like 300.

Since you'll want to be dumping so many points into your Magic total, items which augment other characteristics are almost essential to your well-being. Also, though staffs with high-end spells can really wreak havok about halfway through the game, you'll generally learn the spells you need at some point, and can lay down a staff in lieu of a shield and weapon. If those happen to increase some character trait through magical adjustments, so much the better. Only when you're going to battle a huge hoard, where the Mana cost would be insanely high, should you select a staff for deep in the dungeon. By then, you should have other items which provide significant defensive adjustments that you can be hanging onto: Save the staff for a specific purpose.

Tip

The Damage Done

Early in the game, when you're considering buying or selling magical items, you occasionally have the option between an item that adds a flat adjustment to some attribute, or an item that adjusts the same attribute based on a percentage. When buying from Griswold, he'll put a premium on those items with percentage adjustments, as well he should: In the long run, those are the more valuable. Early in the game, however, a percentage adjustment to your puny totals is, well . . . a smaller percentage of puny. Even though an item with a flat-point adjustment will be priced lower, it'll have a much greater impact on a beginning character's stats than those which feature percentage bonuses.

RANGED ATTACKS

A significant component of *Diablo* combat is the ranged attack, whether that happens to be by bow or magic. As detailed in the previous individual character sections, each class can employ different ranged attack forms to different effect, but there are some general aspects of both physical and magical ranged attacks which you should consider.

MAGICAL COMBAT

The following chapter on Magic and Spells points out some of the specific advantages and disadvantages of particular spells, but magic in general bears a little combat analysis.

In a nutshell, the difference between the three classes when it comes to magic is that the Sorcerer should strive to develop long-range magical attacks, while both the Warrior and Rogue will have to settle for relatively close-combat versions of the high-end spells.

As a combat spell increases in level, it generally increases in area of effect, as well as the economy of Mana with which you can throw the spell. Though a Rogue or Warrior can eventually develop a few of the spells to be on a par with the Sorcerer, the vast majority of prime offensive spells are reserved for the mage, and the significant difference is in the increased area of effect that a high-level Sorcerer produces.

If you're playing the Sorcerer, keep testing out various spells as you climb through experience levels, and you'll be pleasantly surprised at the lists increasing effectiveness. Firebolt, as an example, is a first-level spell that almost every character learns early on. The difference between a Sorcerer's Inferno and that of a Warrior, when both have reached about 20 experience levels, is amazing.

If you're playing the Warrior or Rogue, realize that you're never going to be cutting loose from a distance with magic to devastating effect. Yes, there are some exceptions. In general, you'll find that only lightning-based spells travel a significant distance before dissipating. Even if a creature happens to be lightning resistant, you can still use lightning to soften up a crowd from a distance, and you've probably got the Mana to spare.

Bow Combat

Of specific importance to Rogues will be the proper use of the bow, one of the game's most devastating weapons. Every monster in the dungeon is susceptible to physical harm, and being able to inflict physical, as opposed to magical, damage from a distance is an incredible asset.

Firing the bow effectively is a matter of utilizing the [Shift] key constantly, adjusting your targeting angle without running blindly into the fray.

The problem with bow fighting is the simple act of acquiring the target. In a doorway, that becomes particularly easy, as you can simply highlight the door. When a monster shows up in the portal, it'll highlight automatically, and you can then open fire.

In large and relatively open areas, however, you'll be sweeping you're gauntlet across the crowd to select a target, and most of the time said target won't be nice enough to stay in one place. The danger is that you click on the floor instead of a monster, at which time you begin running forward to the point where you clicked erroneously.

In order to properly acquire a target, hold down the [Shift] key, and begin clicking on the left mouse button. You'll begin to fire arrows, though not with a great deal of accuracy. The trick is to carefully watch your attck angle. A zig-zagging target is much harder to hit then one moving directly toward or away from you, and you'll find that monsters closing the gap are usually easier to hit when moving toward you from the north, south, east, and west (respective to your screen).

Once you've begun firing, and are tracking the target with your gauntlet, you can release the [Shift] key to reposition yourself for a better attack angle. Be mindful that chance To Hit not only is affected by your class but is also affected by your range. The act of firing the weapon will keep you from running forward, and you'll pivot to the proper attack angle.

As you battle with the bow, you'll want to keep one finger near the [Shift] key, alternating between "rooting" yourself in place and releasing the button to adjust your aim ever-so-slightly. Tap the [Shift] key as you fire, and you'll be assured of remaining in one place, while still acquiring targets at sufficient speed. Also, be mindful that your gauntlet is pointing directly at the torso of the monster you're attacking. Simply highlighting the monster isn't enough to ensure a hit.

As a final note, realize that you can hold down the [Shift] key and strafe a large area to wake up the local monsters, if that's your cup of tea. Firing through grates or fences in this manner often initiates several cheap kills, especially when dealing with monsters that can't open a door or gate. Distant monsters, aroused by your arrows, will head over to investigate, and you can pluck at them as they advance, usually polishing off large numbers before they have any chance of counterattack.

MAGICAL RESISTANCES

One of the most significant aspects of solid defense, especially as you delve deeper into the dungeon, is your particular magical resistances. Magic Resistance comes in three types: General, which concerns monsters like the Succubi, and then Fire and Lightning. Just as you face swarms of archers closer to town, the lower you go, the more likely a distance attack is to have some magical component.

The primary thing to realize about magical resistances, aside from the fact that you should get some, is that magical attacks don't damage your armor's Durability the way that physical attacks do. For that reason, you'll occasionally want to outfit yourself based purely on the need for protection from magic, even to the extent of wearing Rags if they come with a significant resistance. Of course, you don't want to sell your good combat armor, but don't be so quick to sell lesser magic items if they boast magical resistance. You're not going to get much gold for them anyway: You might as well leave them up in Tristram until they come in handy. You'll be glad you did, and amazed at the significant amount of protection that magical resistance provides.

WEAPON SELECTION

Once you determine what's on a dungeon level, you must equip your hero (or heroine) accordingly. That includes properly allocating magical items, but in the most basic sense, it means choosing the right weapon for the job.

Briefly, blades (swords) work best on flesh creatures, and clubs, maces, and other blunt instruments are the most effective for breaking up skeletons and the like. The axe combines some of the benefits of both types of weapons (cutting and smashing a foe), but it takes a strong character to wield one effectively. An axe is heavy, requires more time to swing, and you need both hands to control one, precluding the use of a shield. Until you can swing the axe quickly enough to avoid taking disproportionate amounts of damage in return, you should really stick to a sword and shield. Also, an item that has a fast-hit recovery component can add to an axe's overall effectiveness.

The bow is the other significant weapon category, and you would be wise not to overlook it. You need a high Dexterity to use one effectively in standard combat, but any character can fire through a grating and pluck away at a horde of bad guys to good effect. For more bow tips, read the preceding section on Ranged Attacks.

ENTERING LARGE AREAS

Venturing into large, open areas is the *Diablo* equivalent of leaning into a left hook. Sprinting to open that inviting chest innocently at rest in the middle of a room often is tantamount to suicide, especially with an inexperienced character.

Take advantage of the monsters' limited sight range: By slowly creeping forward, you can often coax a few bad guys from a crowd, rather than attract the unwelcome attention of the entire throng.

CROWDED COMBAT

A horde of monsters chasing you through an unfamiliar area is your worst nightmare. Death inevitably follows as you run full-tilt into yet another band of killers. For that reason, proceed carefully, clearing each area so you have room to fall back when you throw open a door and a crowd of critters comes scurrying out.

A monster can choose eight avenues of attack if you're standing in the open. To demonstrate this graphically, place your alter ego in the center of a dungeon room and toss eight similar items into the air around you. They'll fall in a grid pattern around your adventurer—a three-by-three square with you in the center. Rest assured that if eight monsters are swarming at you, every slot will fill with enemies. Even lesser monsters will have eight attacks per round to your one. And, if you survive, it's likely your armor will have peeled off in the process.

STRUCTURAL IMPEDIMENTS

Fortunately, you have better options than standing in the center of a room and getting torn to shreds. First and foremost, try drawing them into the room you just came from.

If you've cleared the dungeon behind you, you needn't worry about finding more of the opposition. The object of your flight is not, of course, to run and hide, but to lie in wait. The monsters are coming; there's no doubt about that.

Use the layout of the dungeon—specifically blind corners and doorways—and the monsters' different movement rates to your advantage. That should be enough.

You'll find that, more often than not, all of one type of monster arrive first. Creatures move at different speeds, and making them come to you effectively decreases the number you must fight at any one time.

You can avoid stepping from behind the corner toward the onrushing evil by holding down the [Shift] key, but read the following tip or you'll end up carving air.

Aside from the common corner, several other structural nuances will inhibit a crowd of monsters. The most obvious are doorways, but killing a monster in a doorway jams the door open for all eternity. That can create problems, but it's often your best option in a pinch. Barrels and grating are also good barriers for ranged combat against creatures without range attacks.

Tip

When you hold down the [Shift] key during combat, your character holds his or her position (as opposed to running in the direction of the targeted enemy). This can be a great help, but it comes with a caveat: Yes, you'll hold your ground, but to an extreme, if you do not track your target with the cursor, you will not pivot effectively. For that reason, once a monster closes to within attack range, it is probably best to *release the* [Shift] *key*; otherwise, the beast frequently leaps behind you while you impotently hack the air where it used to stand.

More Bow Tips

• Know the effective range of your weapon. Although monsters don't seem overly concerned with lobbing projectiles from a considerable distance, you should be. Only the most experienced Rogue has a

CHANCE OF HITTING ANYTHING WITH A BOW
FROM A GREAT DISTANCE AWAY. SURE, ANYONE
CAN GET IN A LUCKY SHOT, BUT WE'RE TALKING
ABOUT KILLING A PACK OF DEMONS HERE. YOU
NEED CONSISTENCY.

- OFTEN, YOU'LL BE ABLE TO SHOOT THROUGH AN
OPENING—A BARRED WINDOW OR THE LIKE—
AND PICK OFF OPPONENTS SAFELY BEFORE YOU
ENTER THEIR ROOM.

- WHEN THE ENEMY IS RETURNING FIRE, AND YOU
DON'T WANT TO PRESS A CLOSE-QUARTERS FIGHT,
TAKE EVASIVE ACTION. MOVE YOUR CHARACTER
A SMALL DISTANCE; CLICK ON THE FLOOR THREE
SQUARES FROM YOUR POSITION. AS YOUR
CHARACTER RUNS, TARGET YOUR NEXT VICTIM.
WITH A LITTLE PRACTICE, YOU CAN BE
HIGHLIGHTING THE TARGET AS YOU REACH YOUR
DESTINATION. SQUEEZE OFF A SHOT, AND THEN
REPEAT THE PROCESS.

The other, somewhat less obvious, impediment is a narrow path between two lava lakes (which become common in the dungeon's cave-like midlevels). Narrower than even a doorway, these are probably the most restrictive hurdles a horde of monsters can run into. If you're tough enough to stand toe-to-toe with one or two foes, you'll win the day. Rogues can hold back and hit the crossing with a hail of arrows. The brutes are slow to form a single-file line, and you should be able to pick them off while they organize.

Mixing Monster Types

Once you begin to encounter more than one type of monster at a time, you'll need to start considering, usually under fire, which type of foe should be your primary target. There are a couple of caveats made for each character class, but there are also some general tactics that serve any adventurer well in those situations.

First, do any of the monsters have ranged attacks? If so, are those attacks physical (arrows) or magical? Finally, how much damage are those distance attackers doing?

If, for instance, you're being attack by archers from a considerable distance, and you're a Warrior with a good armor class and high health, you can almost literally ignore that group of monsters, and deal with any onrushing foe. Analogously, if you're being attacked with magic of a certain type, and you have a very high resistance to that magic, those monsters can remain virtually ignored while you deal with more pressing concerns.

Throughout the levels of dungeon, you'll constantly be tasked with evaluating monsters not just on an individual basis, but also looking at them in particular groups.

As the game gets underway, realize that the monster combos of the first few levels betray a pattern that you'll have to deal with on your entire adventure.

LET THE GAME BEGIN

In the first few levels of the dungeon, you'll encounter a mix of monsters that'll serve you well to study, as many of the different offensive tactics they employ are analogous to others you'll see from tougher foes.

Consider that the Skeletons are middle-of-the road, with an Archer variation. Fallen ones are fast but merely bothersome, while Zombies are slower and can deal out serious damage. In general, you'll deal with Fallen Ones first, since you're hiding from the Archers and the Fallen Ones are the quickest to close the gap. Next come the Skeleton footsoldiers. If Archers show up at the same time, you corner them first. Finally, you double back and look for any Zombies that got away.

Probably the most important characteristic to note of a monster when you first encounter it is its rate of speed, relative to other monsters on that dungeon level. The next consideration is whether or not a monster will chase you after you stick your head in its room. If it doesn't have a ranged attack, the answer is almost always yes. Even if a monster does have a ranged attack, most will pursue, with the lucky exception of the Counselor-type monsters in the depths of hell. Creatures with ranged attacks simply find you and then set up at a certain distance to open fire.

TIP

TOXIC BEASTS

ONE OF THE MORE DANGEROUS MONSTERS YOU'RE LIKELY TO ENCOUNTER WITH A RANGED ATTACK IS THE POISON SPITTER, COMMON IN THE CAVERN DUNGEON LEVELS. USUALLY, THEY SHOW UP WITH MONSTERS THAT ARE GENERALLY SLOWER, BUT THE LAVA LAKES INHIBIT THE POISON SPITTERS' MOVEMENTS SOMEWHAT. TRY TO DRAW OFF THE OTHER MONSTERS WITHOUT INCITING A MAJOR POISON SPITTER SWARM, AND THEN PLUCK AT THE POISON SPITTERS FROM A DISTANCE WITH LIGHTNING. YOU'LL FIND A LIGHTNING BLAST OUTDISTANCES THEIR SPITTING CAPABILITIES. ALSO, NOTE THAT A POISON SPITTER CAN'T OPEN A FENCE. TOO BAD, HUH?

SURVIVING DISTANCE ATTACKS

In all but the Cavern and Hell levels, it's usually feasible to draw a distance attacker through a narrow doorway. Wait on the other side, and take care of business as they file through. Realize that if you're drawing them into another room, they'll attempt to turn and put some distance back between you. Thus, a hallway works best for employing that tactic.

If a ranged attacker won't pursue you into close or confined quarters, and has the added room to run that the Hell or Cavern levels provide, you almost certainly end up dealing with some other monster type first. Draw them to you, away from the incoming aerial assault, and deal with them separately.

Once you've divided the forces, the task of dealing with ranged attackers remains. If you have a bow, that task is a lot easier. If you're playing the Warrior or Sorcerer, the odds are you need a Plan B.

The Sorcerer has to stick to spells that don't dissipate over a distance. Most of those are lightning-based, though Fireball and Elemental also work quite nicely. Check the Spells and Magic chapter for further insights.

A Warrior is in for the roughest road of all when it comes to fighting the large crowds of magical monsters at the bottom of the dungeon. If you're lucky, you'll encounter one type of monster with a distance attack, and another that'll chase after you. Obviously, the monsters which give chase get to feel your blade first.

Past that, the Warrior is going to need some magical resistance, or you'll be using a crazy amount of health just to sustain a relatively short combat. And, if you're chasing around Succubi, there is no such thing as a short combat.

Short of killing high-level ranged attacking monsters from a distance, you have to herd them. The optimum place is the intersection of a hallway with another hall, where the hall being intersected has a dead-end in one direction. Lure the Succubi, or some derivation thereof, into the hall: Run in the opposite direction of the dead-end, against the far wall. The monsters will take up a position against the far wall, just as you did, and begin to fire magic. Now, move to the opposite side of the hallway. If you're following along at home, the door through which you entered the hallway is on this side. Your goal is to move down the hall, towards the monsters, zig-zagging to prevent them from running past you, either on down the hallway or back through the door through which they came: You're herding them into the dead-end.

It takes some practice to learn the movement tendencies of the different monsters, but they all share one common trait: if you get one in a corner, and attack from a 45-degree angle, the monster will stand and slug it out. Even a teleporting monster can be trapped in a corner thus: Just as a monster needs room to run past you, it also needs room to teleport. A teleporting monster can be trapped in a corner, disappearing as usual but reappearing in the exact same place, ripe for the slaughter.

DIABLO'S DENIZENS

Though there are a seemingly endless supply of monster variations in *Diablo*, you'll be heartened to know that there is a finite number. In fact, many of the monsters are derivations of some general type, with added magical immunities, a distance attack perhaps. . . . You get the idea. First, the three basic classes of monsters, followed by specific analysis of each type.

✝ The Undead

This creature class includes Skeletons, Zombies, Ghouls, Rotting Corpses, and all their putrefying brethren. Aside from Holy Bolt or perhaps Fire Magic, tailor your attacks against the abhorred based on specific recommendations for each template in the subsequent section.

DEMONS

This class includes some of the game's most interesting—and deadly—monsters. Demons include Overlords, Magma Demons, Goat Demons, the Hidden, and the Succubi, among a host of other devilish fiends.

These are simply the toughest creatures you'll fight. Smart, quick, and aggressive, many have ranged-attack capability. Only a Warrior with a decent suit of armor and an excellent blade (perhaps an axe?) can stand and slug it out with these guys. A Sorcerer or Rogue should fight them from afar (with a preplanned escape route should the beast close the gap).

ANIMALS

Diablo presents an enormous menagerie of animal-based creatures with a mighty lust for human flesh. Gargoyles, Spitting Terrors, and slavering Scavengers crouch in wait, fangs bared.

Fortunately, animals are vulnerable to almost any form of attack. They make up for this deficiency by showing up in Super-Bowl-attendance–like numbers, and are generally the fleetest foes you'll face. Again, use the dungeon layout to avoid getting swamped, and hammer them into submission.

Monster Index

Diablo's denizens are a diverse lot, yet the vast array of creatures actually derives from a smaller template of monster types. Here's the breakdown, with some observations and recommendations for battling each set. Keep the following definitions in mind when reviewing the data:

- **Resistance:** When a creature is *resistant* to something— magic, fire, or lightning—it can shrug off most of those attacks. If you throw a Charged Bolt at a lightning-resistant creature, you might slow it down, but you probably won't kill it.

- **Immunity:** If a creature is *immune* to your attacks, it is completely unaffected by them. You can shoot Lightning at a lightning-immune demon right up until the point where the monster kills you.

- **Damage:** This number indicates how much hurt the creature will inflict when it strikes.

- **Hit Points:** This number compares to the Hit Points category in the Character Statistics Window. Please be aware that the monsters' Hit Points will all regenerate over time, so you'd better finish them off or you'll be starting from scratch.

- **Armor Class:** This is a measure of how hard it is to hit a monster. The higher the numerical rating, the tougher the beast will be to score a hit on.

ZOMBIES

Slow and deliberate, the tougher versions of the Zombie can nonetheless inflict serious amounts of damage, especially if they swarm on you. Don't let them. With Undead this slow, you should be able to pick your targets one at a time, and take care of business.

TABLE 5-I. ZOMBIES

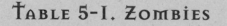

Creature	Category	Resistance	Immunity
Zombie	Undead	0	magic
Ghoul	Undead	0	magic
Rotting Carcass	Undead	0	magic
Black Death	Undead	0	magic

You'll get plenty used to bashing Skeletons.

Experience Gained	Level	Hit Points	Damage	Armor Class
54	1-2	4–7	2–5	5
58	2-3	7–11	3–10	10
136	2-4	7–12	5–15	15
240	3–5	12–20	6–22	20

SKELETONS

Common as roaches, the bony denizens of *Diablo* are best bashed with the nearest blunt instrument. Skeletons are fast, so you'll have to stay mobile while you thin out a crowd, but one hefty blow usually reduces them to dungeon debris.

TABLE 5-2. SKELETONS

Creature	Category	Resistance	Immunity
Skeleton (axe)	Undead	0	magic
Corpse (axe)	Undead	0	magic
Burning Dead (axe)	Undead	fire	magic
Horror (axe)	Undead	lightning	magic
Skeleton (bow)	Undead	0	magic
Corpse (bow)	Undead	0	magic
Burning Dead (bow)	Undead	fire	magic
Horror (bow)	Undead	lightning	magic
Skeleton (captain)	Undead	0	magic
Corpse (captain)	Undead	0	magic
Burning Dead (captain)	Undead	fire	magic
Horror (captain)	Undead	lightning	magic

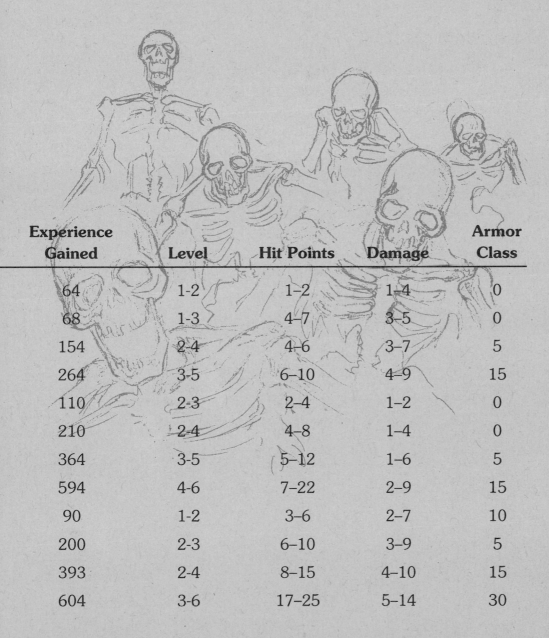

Experience Gained	Level	Hit Points	Damage	Armor Class
64	1-2	1–2	1–4	0
68	1-3	4–7	3–5	0
154	2-4	4–6	3–7	5
264	3-5	6–10	4–9	15
110	2-3	2–4	1–2	0
210	2-4	4–8	1–4	0
364	3-5	5–12	1–6	5
594	4-6	7–22	2–9	15
90	1-2	3–6	2–7	10
200	2-3	6–10	3–9	5
393	2-4	8–15	4–10	15
604	3-6	17–25	5–14	30

FALLEN ONES

The Fallen Ones are the *Diablo* version of the goblin—small, sneaky, and a real pleasure to whack. All but the bravest shriek in terror, turn, and run when they see you slice up a comrade. As long as you keep killing, there's usually no risk of getting swarmed. Large packs, however, deserve respect: The little critters are *fast*.

TABLE 5-3. FALLEN ONES

Creature	Category	Resistance	Immunity
Fallen One (spear)	Animal	0	0
Carver (spear)	Animal	0	0
Devil Kin (spear)	Animal	0	0
Dark One (spear)	Animal	0	0
Fallen One (scimitar)	Animal	0	0
Carver (scimitar)	Animal	0	0
Devil Kin (scimitar)	Animal	0	0
Dark One (scimitar)	Animal	0	0

The Red Death masses at a doorway.

Experience Gained	Level	Hit Points	Damage	Armor Class
46	1-2	1–2	1–3	0
80	2-3	4–8	2–5	5
155	2-4	6–12	3–7	10
255	3-5	10–18	4–8	15
52	1-2	1–2	1–5	10
90	2-3	3–5	2–8	15
180	2-4	8–12	4–10	20
280	3-5	12–18	4–12	25

SCAVENGERS

A link or two up the food chain, so to speak, these are the most common beasts in the dungeon. Small and lightning fast, a group of them can tear you to shreds. Force them to attack you through a narrow opening, and pick them off in small numbers. Otherwise, you're going to get hurt.

TABLE 5-4. SCAVENGERS

Creature	Category	Resistance	Immunity
Scavenger	Animal	0	0
Plague Eater	Animal	0	0
Shadow Beast	Animal	0	0
Bone Gnasher	Animal	magic	0

The Shadow Drinker is a powerful enemy.

Experience Gained	Level	Hit Points	Damage	Armor Class
80	1-2	1–4	1–5	15
188	2-3	6–12	1–8	20
375	2-4	12–18	3–12	25
552	3-5	14–20	5–15	30

THE HIDDEN

The Hidden are an assortment of horrid characters that vanish and reappear a moment before they attack. The tougher the version, the less time you have to react to its appearance before it strikes. You can strike the beasts while they're invisible, but random swinging isn't effective combat. If you have a bow, however, you can take particular pleasure in killing entire hoards before they can even materialize. If you're moving in an open area of dungeon where the monsters might be lurking, move in short, erratic bursts, zig-zagging from side to side in the hall. Pause, then move again a short distance. This method induces these monsters to materialize as soon as you're nearby, and you can attack them one or two at a time. Otherwise, if you traverse an entire hallway without stopping, the entire pack materializes as soon as you make a significant pause. Bad news.

TABLE 5-5. THE HIDDEN

Creature	Category	Resistance	Immunity
Hidden	Demon	0	0
Stalker	Demon	0	0
Unseen	Demon	magic	0
Illusion Weaver	Demon	magic, fire	0

The Illusion Weavers will come at you from all sides.

Experience Gained	Level	Hit Points	Damage	Armor Class
278	2-4	4–12	3–6	25
630	4-6	15–22	8–16	30
935	5-7	17–25	12–20	30
1,500	7-9	40–60	16–24	30

GOAT DEMONS

These folks are common on the mid- to lower lev-els, and commonly show up in mixed groups that include bowmen. By the time Goat Demons show up in large numbers, however, your armor and offensive capabilities should be strong enough to be effective against them. Use the dungeon layout as you would against a pack of Scavengers, and draw the bowmen through a doorway or force them into a corner to keep them in one place for your attack.

TABLE 5-6. GOAT DEMONS

Creature	Category	Resistance	Immunity
Flesh Clan (mace)	Demon	0	0
Stone Clan (mace)	Demon	magic	0
Fire Clan (mace)	Demon	fire	0
Night Clan (mace)	Demon	magic	0
Flesh Clan (bow)	Demon	0	0
Stone Clan (bow)	Demon	magic	0
Fire Clan (bow)	Demon	fire	0
Night Clan (bow)	Demon	magic	0

The Fallen Ones and the Goat Demon will gang up on you in the Poison Water Quest.

Experience Gained	Level	Hit Points	Damage	Armor Class
460	3-5	15–22	4–10	40
685	4-6	20–27	6–12	40
906	5-7	25–32	8–16	45
1190	6-9	27–35	10–20	50
448	3-5	10–17	1–7	35
645	4-6	15–20	2–9	35
822	5-7	20–25	3–11	35
1,092	6-9	25–32	4–13	40

BATS

Another of *Diablo's* more popular creatures, the Bat's small size and swooping attack can be troublesome. They, of course, have a tendency to swarm, and some of the tougher variations can inflict considerable damage that way. Don't hesitate to break off an attack to draw them through a narrower opening so you can pick them off singly.

Bats also have specific attacks depending on their type. The Fiends attack and move away. The Blink Bats will teleport next to you; the Gloom have a charging attack that a quick adventurer can side step; and the Familiars will light you up with a very annoying lightning attack.

TABLE 5-7. BATS

Creature	Category	Resistance	Immunity
Fiend	Animal	0	0
Blink Bat	Animal	0	0
Gloom	Animal	magic	0
Familiar	Animal	magic, lightning	0

Experience Gained	Level	Hit Points	Damage	Armor Class
102	2-3	3–6	1–6	10
340	3-5	6–14	1–8	15
509	4-6	14–18	4–12	35
448	6-8	20–35	4–16	35

ACID BEASTS

Usually the first creature you see with something approximating ranged magic—*Diablo*'s Acid Beasts—are, in some ways, much worse than a creature that fires a simple spell. These monsters vomit a glob of acid, varying in intensity, that damages on contact, and then forms a puddle at your feet. You continue to take damage as you stand in the puddle until the acid dissipates. The acid from the upper-end beasts is so strong, you'll convulse in agony while the fiends spit more goo in your direction. You can fight these beings from a distance, but don't do it standing still. Realize that your Lightning magic provides you with unlimited range, though those poison balls, mercifully, fall to the ground after a certain distance. Even against a Lightning-resistant variation, you can chip away if a horde of these monsters happens to get corraled behind a fence. . . . If you're hacking away at a horde of them, don't let that poison accumulate at your feet. Stay mobile, or die.

TABLE 5-8. ACID BEASTS

Creature	Category	Resistance	Immunity
Acid Beast	Animal	0	0
Poison Spitter	Animal	0	0
Pit Beast	Animal	magic	0
Lava Maw	Animal	magic	fire

Experience Gained	Level	Hit Points	Damage	Armor Class
846	5-7	20–33	4–12	30%
1248	7-9	30–42	4–16	30%
2060	9-11	40–55	8–18	35%
2940	11-14	100–150	10–20	35%

OVERLORDS

The Overlords truly test an adventurer's mettle. Tough as nails and capable of delivering considerable damage, the elite Overlords also resist magical attacks. By the time these guys show up with any regularity, however, you should have at least one semidevastating attack in your bag of tricks. Whatever your ace in the hole, play it when these dark destroyers arrive.

TABLE 5-9. OVERLORDS

Creature	Category	Resistance	Immunity
Overlord	Demon	0	0
Mud Man	Demon	0	0
Toad Demon	Demon	0	magic
Flayed One	demon	magic	fire

The Butcher is an Overlord with an attitude—and a mean cleaver

Experience Gained	Level	Hit Points	Damage	Armor Class
635	4-6	30–40	6–12	55
1,165	6-8	50–62	8–16	60
1,380	8-10	67–80	8–16	65
2058	10-12	80–100	10–20	70

MAGMA DEMONS

These creatures combine demonic durability with the devastating impact of a flaming ranged attack. Again, these creatures show up deep in the dungeon, and by then you should have something sufficiently maleficent to counter them with. Defensively, you must take the edge off their flaming attacks, or you'll be dodging lava balls at an ever-increasing rate. If you don't have some fire resistance by now, it's time to get some. The best tactic is to draw these Demons through a doorway and then unload on them before they get a chance to return the favor. Approach each large area with caution when Magma Demons are present; stick close to the walls to avoid getting drawn into a cross fire.

TABLE 5-10. MAGMA DEMONS

Creature	Category	Resistance	Immunity
Magma Demon	Demon	0	fire, magic
Blood Stone	Demon	0	fire, magic
Hell Stone	Demon	0	fire, magic
Lava Lord	Demon	0	fire, magic

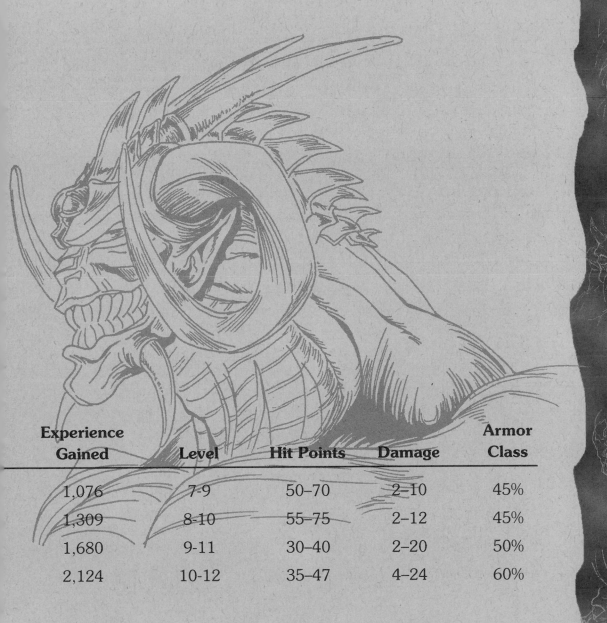

Experience Gained	Level	Hit Points	Damage	Armor Class
1,076	7-9	50–70	2–10	45%
1,309	8-10	55–75	2–12	45%
1,680	9-11	30–40	2–20	50%
2,124	10-12	35–47	4–24	60%

HORNED DEMONS

Not a Demon, thankfully, but an animal, these beings are nonetheless formidable opponents. Their favorite trick is to bend low and charge. If they connect, you can expect a world of hurt. Fortunately, although the charge is rapid, it usually comes from a considerable distance. This normally allows you to step out of the way, get in a couple of hacks, then beat a retreat, mindful that unless you can duck for cover they'll get up to ramming speed once more. You can probably expect these brutes for the first time between dungeon levels 5 and 6.

TABLE 5-11. HORNED DEMONS

Creature	Category	Resistance	Immunity
Horned Demon	Animal	0	0
Mud Runner	Animal	0	0
Frost Charger	Animal	lightning	magic
Obsidian Lord	Animal	lightning	magic

The Horned Demons are the bane of the Catacombs.

Experience Gained	Level	Hit Points	Damage	Armor Class
1,172	6-8	20–40	2–16	40%
1,404	7-9	50–90	6–18	45%
1,720	8-10	60–100	8–20	50%
1,809	9-12	70–110	10–22	55%

RED STORM

Your first taste of Lightning will most likely come at the hands of these entities, and you'll need some means of Lightning resistance to be effective against them in battle. Not particularly tough in close combat, they do possess a resistance to Magic and an immunity to Lightning that can make a Sorcerer's life difficult. If, as a Sorcerer, you haven't developed some alternative to your lightening attacks, you'll soon wish you'd been more prudent.

TABLE 5-12. RED STORM

Creature	Category	Resistance	Immunity
Red Storm	Demon	light	magic
Storm Rider	Demon	magic	lightning
Storm Lord	Demon	magic	lightning
Maelstrom	Demon	magic	lightning

Experience Gained	Level	Hit Points	Damage	Armor Class
2,160	9-11	55–110	8–18	30%
2,391	10-12	60–120	8–18	30%
2,775	11-13	75–135	12–24	35%
3,177	12-14	90–150	15–28	40%

Gargoyles

Gargoyles are some of the most frustrating denizens of the dungeon. Tough to hit and having a strong attack, they show up in flocks, disguised as statues until your presence alerts them. As you encounter these beasts, sweep the gauntlet cautiously over darkened areas in rooms and hallways to outline them. They'll sit immobile in the dark, and, though they often possess magical immunities, you can roust them individually with a concentrated blast of magic. Once a single gargoyle is in the air, it'll fly over to you, allowing you to deal one-on-one as opposed to alerting the entire flock of the savage creatures. You can also creep forward until a couple take flight due to your proximity. Inadvertently roust a whole pack of Gargoyles, and you've got problems. They're slow to follow you through doorways, and entering a room full of alerted Gargoyles is a very bad idea, so in that instance you might as well wait outside and attack them as they emerge.

Table 5-13. Gargoyles

Creature	Category	Resistance	Immunity
Winged Demon	Demon	0	fire, magic
Gargoyle	Demon	0	light, magic
Blood Claw	Demon	0	magic, fire
Death Wing	Demon	0	magic, light

Experience Gained	Level	Hit Points	Damage	Armor Class
662	4-6	45–60	10–16	45
1,205	6-8	60–90	10–16	45
1,873	8-10	75–125	14–22	50
2278	9-11	90–150	16–28	60

BALROGS

Some of the toughest villains in the game, the Balrogs mean business. With Hit Points and Armor Class comparable to your own, as well as magic resistance and immunity to fire-based attacks, you'll need a ranged attack of the devastating, nonflaming variety. Try a few bursts of chain lightning, or perhaps (if you're lucky) the Stone Curse. If you must go toe to toe, be ready to beat a hasty retreat if a Balrog seizes the initiative. You won't be able to withstand his onslaught for long.

TABLE 5-14. BALROGS

Creature	Category	Resistance	Immunity
Slayer	Demon	magic	fire
Guardian	Demon	magic	fire
Vortex Lord	Demon	magic	fire
Balrog	Demon	magic	fire

*The Balrogs will give you reason enough
to seek fire resistance.*

Experience Gained	Level	Hit Points	Damage	Armor Class
2,300	10-12	60–100	12–20	70
2,714	11-13	75–112	14–26	80
3,252	12-13	87–125	18–36	85
643	13-15	100–150	22–40	90

VIPERS

The slithering Vipers are widespread in the lower levels of the dungeon. Their strength lies in numbers. Pick them off one or two at a time, or they'll overwhelm you like the pack beasts of the upper-level dungeons. Note the various magical resistances and immunities.

TABLE 5-15. VIPERS

Creature	Category	Resistance	Immunity
Cave Viper	Demon	0	magic
Fire Drake	Demon	fire	magic
Gold Viper	Demon	lighting	magic
Azure Drake	Demon	fire,lightning	0

Experience Gained	Level	Hit Points	Damage	Armor Class
2,725	10-12	100–150	8–20	60
3,139	11-13	120–170	12–24	65
3,540	12-14	140–180	15–26	70
3,791	14-15	160–200	18–30	75

Knights

Blizzard provided the Knights to make your life interesting and its continuance uncertain. Found near the bottom of the *Diablo* dungeon, Knights resist virtually every type of magic and possess hundreds of Hit Points and armor that rivals your own. The best strategy is to retreat and pick them off one at a time. Two or more attacking on you is a no-win proposition, and only the bravest Warrior, with a vicious weapon in hand, can go toe to toe with one. Having some kind of a fast-attack or fast-hit recovery bonus makes dealing with these villains significantly easier, so don't overlook that aspect when configuring for combat.

TABLE 5-16. Knights

Creature	Category	Resistance	Immunity
Black Knight	Demon	lightning, magic	0
Doom Guard	Demon	fire, magic	0
Steel Lord	Demon	lightning, magic	fire
Blood Knight	Demon	fire	lightning, magic

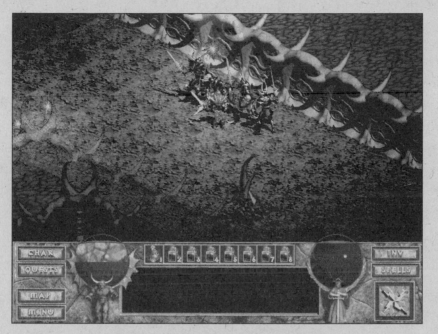

The Steel Lords are tough and deadly deep-level demons.

Experience Gained	Level	Hit Points	Damage	Armor Class
3,360	11-13	150	15–20	75
3,650	13-14	165	18–25	75
4,252	14-15	180	20–30	80
5,130	15-16	200	25–35	85

SUCCUBI

The Succubi patrol the depths of the dungeon in packs, sending streams of magic in your direction. To defeat them you'll need a wicked ranged attack, or some serious magic resistance. Though a Warrior may be able to herd a pack into a corner and take care of business, a Sorcerer will almost certainly want a staff in hand, to deliver damage without burning Mana. Without a staff and some resistance, the Sorcerer is in for a tedious game of cat-and-mouse, or will at least be using a lot of gold to stock up on Mana.

TABLE 5-17. SUCCUBI

Creature	Category	Resistance	Immunity
Succubus	Demon	magic	0
Snow Witch	Demon	lightning	0
Hell Spawn	Demon	magic	lightning
Soul Burner	Demon	magic, lightning	fire

Experience Gained	Level	Hit Points	Damage	Armor Class
3,696	11-13	120–150	1–20	60
4,084	12-13	135–175	1–24	65
4,480	13-14	150–200	1–30	75
4,644	15-16	140–225	1–35	85

COUNSELORS

The entrée on the monster menu is the magical, teleporting set of Counselors. You'll need healthy magic resistance (in general, or lightning specifically) to combat these horrors. As strange as it sounds, it's often best to fight from close quarters, especially if you're the Warrior. The Counselors don't have a lot of Hit Points, although they'll often seize the initiative when you close the gap. If that seems to be the case, quickly break off the fight and rejoin it at close quarters. If you can land the first blow, you can usually get in a couple more to finish

ϮABLE 5-18. COUNSELORS

Creature	Category	Resistance	Immunity
Counselor	Demon	magic, lightning, fire	0
Magistrate	Demon	magic, lightning	fire
Cabalist	Demon	magic, fire	lightning
Advocate	Demon	fire	lightning, magic

the job. The Counselors' various resistances mean Sorcerer and Rogue have an uphill battle. You'll probably burn more Mana than seems reasonable to finish these guys off, and you'll need to be highly resistant to the Counselor's attacks to survive. Realize that you can track a Counselor even when he's teleporting by watching the light patterns on the floor. The instant he begins to materialize, you can be acquiring the target, whether that's to take a swing with a sword or to unleash an arrow or magical attack.

Experience Gained	Level	Hit Points	Damage	Armor Class
4,070	12-13	70	8–20	0
4,478	13-14	85	10–24	0
4,929	14-15	120	14–30	0
4,968	16	145	15–25	0

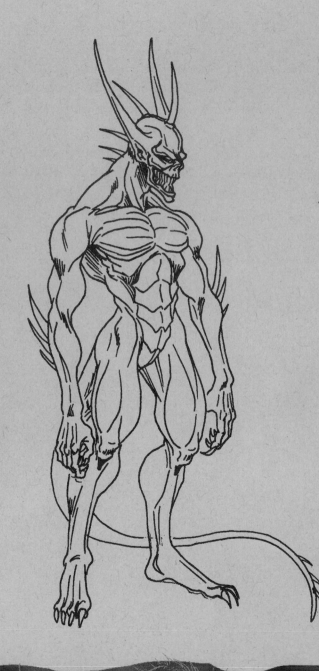

Unique Monsters

Beyond the basic monster categories, the game randomly throws in what the developers call "Uniques." These named monsters are devastating versions of their brethren, usually resembling them except for their coloring or armaments, and packing much more of a punch. The experience given for Uniques is approximately double that for monsters of their type. They also have more immunities, are more resistant to your attacks, and do more damage, although they maintain a similar Armor Class.

Often, Uniques will be surrounded by their more ordinary siblings, who'll be far more dangerous than usual. The reason is that a Unique imbues its horde with whatever specific magic ability is at he Unique's disposal, from modes of attack to invisibility. Take out the Unique quickly if at all possible when this happens, and the minions will lose that special ability.

The good news is that slaying a Unique yields a magical item, so at least there's a significant reward for your trouble. Here's the complete list of the Uniques.

TABLE 5-19. UNIQUES

Name	Basic Creature Type	Level
Bonehead Keenaxe	Corpse axe	2
Bladeskin the Slasher	Fallen scimitar	2
Soulpus	Zombie	2
Pukerat the Unclean	Fallen spear	2
Boneripper	Skeleton axe	2
Rotfeast the Hungry	Zombie	2
Gutshank the Quick	Carver scimitar	3
Bonehead Bangshield	Corpse captain	3
Bongo	Devil Kin spear	3
Rotcarnage	Ghoul	3
Shadowbite	Scavenger	2
Deadeye	Skeleton archer	2
Madeye the Dead	Burning Dead axe	4
El Chupacabra	Plague Eater	3
Skullfire	Corpse archer	3
Warpskull	Hidden	3
Goretongue	Rotting Corpse	3
Pulsecrawler	Shadow Beast	4
Snotspill	Dark One (scimitar)	4
Gharbad the Weak	Flesh Clan (mace)	4
Wrathraven	Blink Bat	4

Hit Points	Damage	Resistance	Immunity
91	4–10	0	0
51	6–18	fire	0
133	4–8	fire, lightning	0
77	1–5	fire	0
54	6–15	0	fire
85	4–12	0	0
66	6–16	fire	0
108	12–20	lightning	
178	9–21	0	0
102	9–24	lightning	0
60	3–20	0	fire
49	6–9	fire	0
75	9–21	lightning, fire, magic	0
120	10–18	fire	0
125	6–10	0	fire
117	6–18	fire, lightning	0
156	15–30	0	0
150	16–20	lightning	fire
220	10–18	lightning	0
120	8–16	0	0
135	9–27	0	fire

TABLE 5-19. UNIQUES

Name	Basic Creature Type	Level
Moonbender	Bat	4
Zhar the Mad	Counselor	8
Spineeater	Bone Gnasher	4
Blackash the Burning	Burning Dead (archer)	4
Shadowcrow	Dark One (scimitar)	5
Bloodskin Darkbrow	Flesh Clan (bow)	5
Foulwing	Gloom Fang	5
Shadowdrinker	Horror (captain)	5
Hazeshifter	Unseen	5
Bilefroth the Pit Master	Overlord	6
Deathspit	Acid Beast	6
Bloodgutter	Fire Clan (mace)	6
Deathshade Fleshmaul	Stone Clan (mace)	6
Glasskull the Jagged	Red Storm	7
Blightfire	Fire Clan (bow)	7
Nightwing the Cold	Gargoyle	7
Gorestone Deatharrow	Night Clan (bow)	7
Blighthorn Steelmace	Night Clan (mace)	7
Bronzefist Firestone	Hell Stone	8
Firewound the Grim	Magma	8
Baron Sludge	Mudman	8

Hit Points	Damage	Resistance	Immunity
135	9–27	0	fire
360	16–40	fire, lightning	magic
180	18–25	0	lightning
120	6–16	lightning	0
270	12–25	0	0
207	3–16	fire, lightning	
246	12–28	fire	0
300	18–26	fire, lightning	0
285	18–30	0	lightning
210	16–23	0	0
303	12–32	lightning	0
315	24–34	0	fire
276	12–24	fire	magic
354	18–30	0	fire, magic
321	13–21	0	fire
342	18–26	lightning	magic
303	15–28	lightning	0
250	20–28	lightning	0
360	30–36	fire	magic
303	18–22	fire	0
315	25–34	lightning	magic

TABLE 5-19. UNIQUES

Name	Basic Creature Type	Level
Chaoscrawler	Poison Spitter	8
Breakspine the Cruel	Mud Runner	9
Devilskull Sharpbone	Red Death	9
Brokenstorm	Red Storm	9
Stormbane	Storm Rider	9
Oozedrool	Toad Demon	9
Goldblight of the Flame	Bloodclaw	10
Blackstorm	Obsidian Lord	10
Plaguewrath	Pit Beast	10
The Flayer	Storm Rider	10
Bluehorn	Frost Charger	11
Fangspeir	Cave Viper	11
Lionskull the Bent	Black Knight	12
Blacktongue	Counselor	12
Viletouch	Death Wing	12
Viperflame	Fire Drake	12
Fangskin	Gold Magi	12
Witchfire the Unholy	Succubus	12
Lord of the Pit	Cave Viper	13

Hit Points	Damage	Resistance	Immunity
240	12–20	lightning	
351	25–34	fire	0
444	25–40	0	fire
411	25–36	0	lightning
555	30–30	0	lightning
483	25–30	lightning	0
405	15–35	0	fire, magic
525	20–40	0	lightning
450	20–30	fire	magic
501	25–35	fire, magic	lightning
477	25–30	fire	magic
444	15–32	fire, lightning	0
525	25–25	lightning	fire, magic
360	15–30	fire	0
525	20–40	fire	lightning
570	25–35	lightning	fire
681	50–50	fire, lightning	magic
444	10–20	lightning	fire, magic
762	25–42	fire	0

TABLE 5-19. UNIQUES

Name	Basic Creature Type	Level
Rustweaver	Doom Guard	13
Doomcloud	Maelstrom	13
Witchmoon	Snow Witch	13
Gorefeast Angelkiller	Vortex Lord	13
Graywar the Slayer	Doom Guard	14
Dreadjudge	Magistrate	14
Stareye the Witch	Hell Spawn	14
Steelskull the Hunter	Steel Lord	14
Lachdanan	Black Knight	14
Warlord of Blood	Black Knight	14
Sir Gorash	Blood Knight	15
The Vizier	Cabalist	15
Bloodlust	Hell Spawn	15
Archbishop Lazarus	Advocate	15
Webwidow	Hell Spawn	16
Fleshdancer	Soul Burner	16
Red Vex	Hell Spawn	endgame
Black Jade	Hell Spawn	endgame
Diablo	Lord of Terror	16

Hit Points	Damage	Resistance	Immunity
400	1–60	fire, lightning, magic	0
612	1–60	fire	lightning
310	30–40	fire	0
771	20–30	fire, lightning	0
672	30–50	lightning	0
540	30–40	fire, lightning	magic
726	30–50	0	fire
831	40–50	lightning	0
500	N/A	N/A	N/A
500	N/A	N/A	N/A
1,050	20–60	0	0
850	25–40	0	fire, lightning
825	20–55	0	lightning, magic
600	30–50	fire, lightning	potions, magic
774	20–50	0	fire, magic
999	30–50	fire	potions, magic
400	30–50	fire	magic
400	30–50	lightning	magic
1,666	30–60	fire, lightning	magic

6

WEAPONS,
ARMOR, AND
OTHER
TREASURES

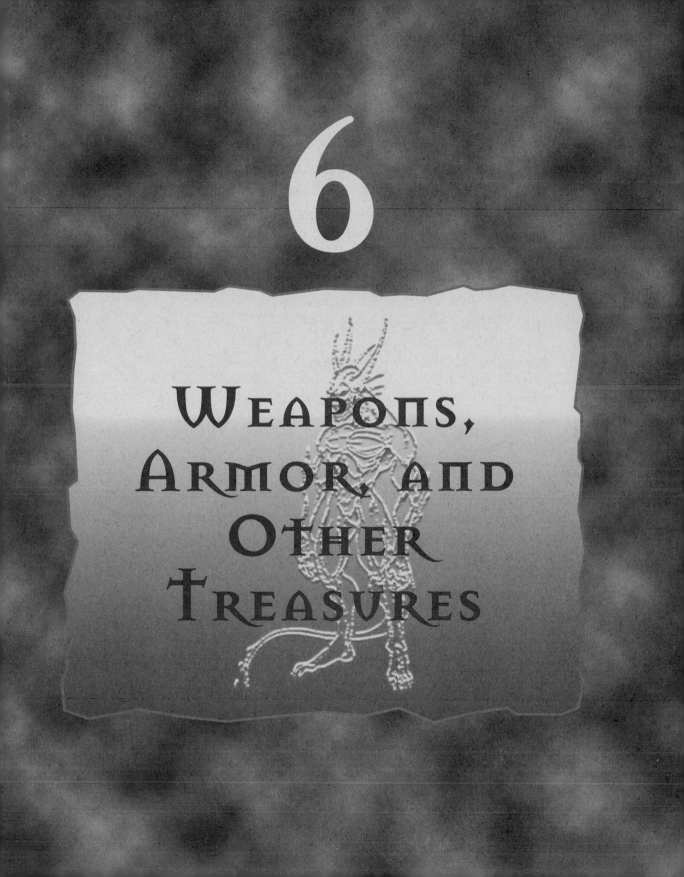

One of the best things about *Diablo* is the seemingly endless variety of arms and equipment the game provides. Every level offers interesting items you'll likely never run into again, no matter how often you play the game, due to the innovative system by which arms and treasures get magical properties.

The game manual does a good job of explaining the basic types of weapons and armor. (Tables are included for particular items later in this chapter.) Alongside basic variables for Attack Damage and Durability lies what may be the game's most intriguing component: Assigning magical properties using prefixes and suffixes.

THE BEGINNING AND THE ENDING

When you acquire a magical item in *Diablo*—whether weapon, armor, amulet, or cloak—a set of randomly assigned prefixes and suffixes defines its properties. The list itself is impressive. The possible combinations are overwhelming.

Here are the complete lists of prefixes and suffixes. Obviously, items that come with both prefix and suffix—assuming they're positive attributes—are best. Tables for basic weapon attributes follow, for those of you into such mundane number-crunching. . . .

Table 6-1. Prefixes

Prefix	Effect
Amber	+16% to +20% Resist All
Angel's	all spells up one level
Arch-Angels'	all spells up two levels
Awesome	+131% to +150% Armor
Azure	+21% to 30% Resist Lightning
Bent	-50% to -75% Damage
Blessed	+91% to +110% Armor
Blue	+10% to +20% Resist Lightning
Bountiful	charges tripled
Brass	-1 to -5 To Hit
Bronze	+1 to +5 To Hit
Brutal	+81% to +95% Damage
Burgundy	+31% to +40% Resist Fire
Champion's	+126% to +150% Damage and +51 to +75 To Hit
Clumsy	-50% to -75% Damage and -1 to -5 To Hit
Cobalt	+41% to +50% Resist Lightning
Crimson	+21% to +40% Resist Fire
Crystal	+41% to +50% Resist General Magic
Deadly	+36% to +50% Damage
Diamond	+51% to +60% Resist General Magic

Prefix	Effect
Dragon's	+51 to +60 Mana
Drake's	+41 to +50 Mana
Dull	-25% to -45% Damage and -4 to -5 To Hit
Emerald	+41% to +50% Resist All
Fine	+20% to +30% armor
Frog's	-1 to -10 Mana
Garnet	+41% to +50% Resist Fire
Glorious	+71% to +90% Armor
Godly	+171% to +200% Armor
Gold	+21 to +30 To Hit
Heavy	+51% to +65% Damage
Holy	+151% to 170% Armor
Hyena's	-11 to -25 Mana
Hydra's	+81 to +100 Mana
Iron	+6 to +10 To Hit
Ivory	+31% to +40% Resist General Magic
Jade	+21% to +30% Resist All
Jagged	+20% to +35% Damage
King's	+151% to +175% Damage and +76 to +100 To Hit
Knight's	+96% to +110% Damage and +31 to +40 To Hit
Lapis	+31% to 40% Resist Lightning

Prefix	Effect
Lord's	Damage +81% to +95% and +21 to +30 To Hit
Massive	+96 % to +110% Damage
Master's	+111% to +125& Damage and +41 to +50 To Hit
Grand	+41% to +55% Armor
Mithril	+41 to +60 To Hit
Merciless	+151% to +175% Damage
Meteoric	+61 to +80 To Hit
Obsidian	+31% to +40% Resist All
Pearl	+21% to +30% Resist General Magic
Platinum	+31 to +40 To Hit
Plentiful	charges doubled
Raven's	+16 to +20 Mana
Red	+10% to +20% Resist Fire
Ruby	+51% to 60% Resist Fire
Rusted	-25% to -50% Armor
Ruthless	+126% to +150% Damage
Saintly	+111% to +130% Armor
Sapphire	+51% to +60% Resist Lightning
Savage	+111% to +125% Damage
Serpent's	+30 to +40 Mana
Sharp	+20% to +35% Damage and +1 to +5 To Hit

Prefix	Effect
Silver	+16 to +20 To Hit
Snake's	+21 to +30 Mana
Soldier's	+66% to +80% Damage +16 to +20 To Hit
Spider's	+10 to +15 Mana
Steel	+11 to +15 To Hit
Strong	+31% to +40% Armor
Strange	+101 to +150 To Hit
Sturdy	+20% to +30% Armor
Tin	-6 to-10 To Hit
Topaz	+10% to +15% Resist All
Useless	-100% Damage
Valiant	+56% to +70% Armor
Vicious	+66% to +80% Damage
Vulnerable	-51% to -100% Armor
Warrior's	+51% to +65% Damage and +11 to +15 To Hit
Weak	-25% to -45% Damage
Weird	+81 to +100 To Hit
White	+10% to +20% Resist General Magic
Wyrm's	+61 to +80 Mana

Table 6-2. Suffixes

Suffix	Effect
of Absorption	-3 Hit Points per hit received, hand-to-hand only
of Accuracy	+11 to +15 Dexterity
of the Ages	Indestructible
of Atrophy	-1 to -5 Dexterity
of Balance	skip frame 2 of "get hit"
of Bashing	each hit removes 8 to 24 points from target's Armor class
of the Bat	adds 3% Damage done to Mana
of the Bear	knocks monster back (if possible) one square
of Blocking	skip all frames of "get hit" but frame 1 of "block"
of Blood	adds 6% Damage done to Life
of Brilliance	+11 to +15 Magic
of Brittleness	-26% to -75% Durability
of Burning	fire arrow (+1 to +16 Fire Damage)
of Carnage	+13 to +16 Damage
of Corruption	lose all Mana
of Craftsmanship	+51% to +100% Durability
of the Crusaders	50% last attack's Damage added to next attack
of the Dark	-4 squares of Light Radius
of Dexterity	+1 to +5 Dexterity

Suffix	Effect
of Disease	-1 to -5 Vitality
of Dyslexia	-1 to -5 Magic
of the Eagle	+21 to +30 Hit Points
of Fire	fire arrow (+1 to +6 Fire Damage)
of Flame	fire arrow (+1 to +3 Fire Damage)
of the Fool	-6 to +10 Magic
of the Fox	+10 to +15 Hit Points
of Fragility	only 1 point of durability
of Frailty	-6 to -10 Strength
of the Giant	+16 to +20 Strength
of Gore	+9 to +12 Damage
of Harmony	skip frames 2, 4, and 6 of "get hit"
of Haste	skip frames 1, 2, 4, and 5 of attack animation
of Health	-1 Hit Point per hit received, hand-to-hand only
of the Heavens	+12 to +15 all stats
of Illness	-6 to -10 Vitality
of the Jackal	-1 to -10 Hit Points
of the Jaguar	+16 to +20 Hit Points
of the Leech	adds 3% Damage done to Life
of Life	-4 to Hit Points per hit received, hand-to-hand only
of Light	+2 squares of Light Radius

Suffix	Effect
of Lightning	lightning arrow (+1 to +10 Lightning Damage)
of the Lion	+51 to +60 Hit Points
of Magic	+1 to +5 Magic
of Maiming	+3 to +5 Damage
of the Mammoth	+61 to +80 Hit Points
of Many	+100% arrows (Durability)
of Might	+6 to +10 Strength
of the Mind	+6 to +10 Magic
of the Moon	+4 to +7 all stats
of the Night	-2 squares of Light Radius
of the Pit	-1 to -5 all stats
of Quality	+1 to +2 Damage
of Radiance	+4 squares of Light Radius
of Tears	+1 Hit Point per hit received, hand-to-hand only
of the Thief	Trap Damage is cut by half
of Thunder	lightning arrow (+1 to +20 Lightning Damage)
of the Tiger	+41 to +50 Hit Points
of the Titan	+21 to +30 Strength
of Trouble	-6 to -10 all stats
of Osmosis	-5 to -6 Hit Points per hit received, hand-to-hand only

Suffix	Effect
of Pain	+2 to +4 Hit Points per hit received, hand-to-hand only
of Paralysis	-6 to -10 Dexterity
of Perfection	+21 to +30 Dexterity
of Piercing	each hit removes 2 to 6 points from target's Armor class
of Plenty	+200% arrows (Durability)
of Power	+11 to +15 Strength
of Precision	+16 to +20 Dexterity
of Protection	-2 Hit Points per hit received, hand-to-hand only
of Puncturing	each hit removes 4 to 12 points from target's Armor class
of Readiness	skip frame 1 of attack animation
of Shock	lightning arrow (+1 to +6 Lightning Damage)
of Skill	+6 to +10 Dexterity
of the Sky	+1 to +3 all stats
of Slaughter	+17 to +20 Damage
of Slaying	+6 to +8 Damage
of Sorcery	+16 to +20 Magic
of Speed	skip frames 1, 3, and 5 of attack animation
of Stability	skip frames 2 and 4 of "get hit"
of the Stars	+8 to +11 all stats
of Structure	+101% to +200% Durability

Suffix	Effect
of Sturdiness	+26% to +50% Durability
of Strength	+1 to +5 Strength
of Spikes	attacking monster takes 1-10 Damage if it hits
of Swiftness	skip frames 1 and 3 of attack animation
of Thorns	attacking monster takes 1-6 Damage if it hits
of the Vampire	adds 6% Damage done to Mana
of Vigor	+16 to +20 Vitality
of Vileness	the monster you hit won't heal
of Vim	+11 to +15 Vitality
of Vitality	+1 to +5 Vitality
of the Vulture	-11 to -25 Hit Points
of Weakness	-1 to -5 Strength
of the Whale	+81 to +100 Hit Points
of Wizardry	+21 to +30 Magic
of the Wolf	+30 to +40 Hit Points
of Zest	+6 to +10 Vitality
of the Zodiac	+16 to +20 all stats

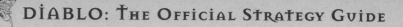

BASIC WEAPONS AND ARMOR

Now that all that fun stuff is out of the way, here's a little more common grist for the mill. The following tables list the attributes for weapons and armor that come without a magical component.

TABLE 6-3. HELMS

Helm	Cost	Durability
Cap	15	15
Skull Cap	40	20
Helm	100	30
Full Helm	250	35
Great Helm	500	60
Crown	1000	40

TABLE 6-4. ARMOR

Armor	Cost	Durability
Cape	20	12
Rags	10	6
Cloak	50	18
Robe	100	24
Quilted Armor	250	30

Requirements	Level	Damage	Armor Class
0	1	0	1–2
0	2	0	2–4
25str	4	0	4–6
35str	6	0	6–8
50str	8	0	8–12
40str	10	0	10–15

Requirements	Level	Damage	Armor Class
0	1	0	1–5
0	1	0	2–6
0	1	0	2–7
0	2	0	4–7
0	2	0	7–10

Armor	Cost	Durability
Leather Armor	335	35
Hard Leather Armor	500	40
Studded Leather	750	45
Ring Mail	1000	50
Chain Mail	1500	55
Scale Mail	2500	60
Breast Plate	3000	80
Splint Mail	3500	65
Plate Mail	5000	75
Field Plate	6000	80
Gothic Plate	10000	100
Full Plate Mail	7500	90

TABLE 6-5. SHIELDS

Shield	Cost	Durability
Buckler	50	16
Small Shield	100	24
Large Shield	250	32
Kite Shield	500	40
Tower Shield	1000	50
Gothic Shield	2500	60

Requirements	Level	Damage	Armor Class
0	3	0	10–13
0	3	0	11–14
20str	4	0	15–17
25str	5	0	17–20
30str	6	0	18–22
35str	7	0	23–2
40str	8	0	20–24
45str	8	0	30–35
60str	9	0	42–50
65str	10	0	40–45
80str	11	0	50–60
90str	12	0	60–75

Requirements	Level	Damage	Armor Class
0	1	0	3-5
25str	2	0	5–8
40str	4	0	8–11
50str	7	0	11–15
60str	10	0	15–20
80str	11	0	14–18

TABLE 6-6. SWORDS

Sword	Cost	Durability
Dagger	60	16
Short Sword	120	24
Falchion	250	20
Scimitar	200	28
Claymore	450	36
Blade	280	30
Sabre	170	45
Long Sword	350	40
Broad Sword	750	50
Bastard Sword	1000	60
Two-Handed Sword	1800	75
Great Sword	3000	100

TABLE 6-7. AXES

Axe	Cost	Durability
Small Axe	100	24
Axe	220	32
Large Axe	850	40
Broad Axe	1100	50
Battle Axe	1500	60
Great Axe	2500	75

Requirements	Level	Damage	Armor Class
0	1	1–4	0
18str	1	2–6	0
30str	2	4–8	0
23str, 23dex	4	3–7	0
35str	5	1–12	0
25str, 30dex	4	2–8	0
17str	1	1–8	0
30str, 30dex	6	2–10	0
40str	8	4–12	0
50str	10	6–15	0
65str	14	8–16	0
75str	17	10–20	0

Requirements	Level	Damage	Armor Class
0	2	2–10	0
22str	4	4–12	0
30str	8	6–16	0
50str	11	8–20	0
65str	14	10–25	0
80str	18	12–30	0

TABLE 6-8. CLUBS

Club	Cost	Durability
Mace	200	32
Morning Star	300	40
War Hammer	600	50
Club	20	20
Spiked Club	60	20
Flail	500	36
Maul	900	50

TABLE 6-9. BOWS

Bow	Cost	Durability
Short Bow	100	30
Hunter's Bow	350	40
Long Bow	250	35
Composite Bow	600	45
Short Battle Bow	1000	45
Long Battle Bow	1500	50
Short War Bow	2000	55
Long War Bow	2500	60

Requirements	Level	Damage	Armor Class
16str	2	1–8	0
26str	3	1–10	0
40str	5	5–9	0
0	1	1–6	0
18str	4	3–6	0
30str	7	2–12	0
55str	10	6–20	0

Requirements	Level	Damage	Armor Class
0	1	1–4	0
20str, 35dex	3	2–5	0
25str, 30dex	3	1–6	0
25str, 40dex	7	3–6	0
30str, 50dex	9	3–7	0
30str, 60dex	11	1–10	0
35str, 70dex	15	4–8	0
45str, 80dex	19	1–14	0

TABLE 6-10. STAFFS

Staff	Cost	Durability
Short Staff	30	25
Long Staff	100	35
Composite Staff	500	45
Battle Staff	1000	55
War Staff	1500	75

Requirements	Level	Damage	Armor Class
0	1	2–4	0
0	4	4–8	0
0	6	5–10	0
20str	9	6–12	0
30str	12	8–16	0

UNIQUE WEAPONS

Diablo's armory also includes a variety of unique weapons and armor, one-of-a-kind pieces that show up at unpredictable times and places. Some of this weaponry appears when you slay Unique monsters; other pieces appear only when you complete the quests. Table 6-11 lists these unique weapons and their capabilities. Note them carefully; some of these armaments actually *reduce* your effectiveness in combat.

TABLE 6-11. UNIQUE WEAPONS

Unique Weapon	Type	Attributes/Actions
The Rift Bow	Short Bow	arrow flies at random speed (real slow to real fast), +2 damage, -3 DEX
The Needler	Short Bow	+50% to hit, does 1-3 damage
The Blackoak Bow	Long Bow	+10 Dex, -10 Vit, +50% damage, -10% light radius
Flamedart	Bow	Fire arrow, +1to6 fire dam, +20% to hit, resist fire 40%
Fleshstinger	Long Bow	+15 DEX, +40% to hit, +80% damage, 6 durability
Windforce	Long War Bow	+5 STR, +200% damage, knockback (of the Bear)

Unique Weapon	Type	Attributes/Actions
Eaglehorn	Long Battle Bow	+20 DEX, +50% to hit, +100% damage, indestructible
Gonnagal's Dirk	Dagger	-5 DEX, +4 damage, fast attack, +25% resist fire
The Defender	Sabre	Adds 5 to AC, +5 VIT, -5 to damage received
Gryphon's Claw	Falchion	+100% to damage, -2 MAG, -5 DEX
Black Razor	Dagger	+150% to damage, +2 VIT, Durability=5
Gibous Moon	Broadsword	+2 to all stats, +25% to damage, +15 mana, decreases light radius 30%
Ice Shank	Long Sword	resist fire 40%, Drability=15, Str +5-10
The Executioner's Blade	Falchion	+150% damage, -10 HP, -10% light radius, +200% durability
The Bonesaw	Claymore	+10 damage, +10 STR, -5 MAG, -5 DEX, +10 HP, -10 Mana
Shadowhawk	Broad Sword	-20% light radius, steals 5% mana, +15 to hit, +5 resist all
Wizardspike	Dagger	+15 MAG, +35 Mana, +25% to hit, +15% resist all

Unique Weapon	Type	Attributes/Actions
Lightsabre	Sabre	+ 20% light radius, +1 to +10 lightning damage, +20% to hit, +50% resist lightning
The Falcon's Talon	Scimitar	+20% to hit, -33% damage, +10% Dex, Fastest Attack
Inferno	Long Sword	+2 to +12 fire damage, +30% light radius, +20 Mana, +80% resist fire
Doombringer	Bastard Sword	+25% to hit, +250% damage, -5 all STATS, -20% light radius, -25 HP
The Grizzly	Two-handed Sword durability	+20% STR, -5 VIT, +200% damage, knockback, +100%
The Grandfather	Great Sword	1 handed, +5 to all STATS, +20 to hit, +70% damage, +20 HP,
The Mangler	Large Axe	+200% damage, -5DEX, -5 MAG, -10 mana
Sharp Beak	Large Axe	+20 HP, -10 MAG, -10 Mana
Bloodslayer	Broad Axe	+100% damage, +50% damage to demons, -5 to all stats, -1 to all spell levels
The Celestial Axe	Battle Axe	No STR requirement, +15% to hit, +15 HP, -15 STR
Wicked Axe	Large Axe	+30 to hit, +10 Dex, -10 VIT, -1 to 6 to damage received

Unique Weapon	Type	Attributes/Actions
Stonecleaver	Broad Axe	+30 HP, +20% to hit, +50% damage, +40 resist lightning
Aguinara's Hatchet	Small Axe	+10 MAG, +80% resist magic, all spells up 1 level
Hellslayer	Battle Axe	+8 STR, +8 VIT, +100% damage, +25HP, -25Mana
Messerschmidt's Reaver	Great Axe	+200% damage, +15 to damage, +5 to all stats, -50 HP, fire hit (2-12)
Crackrust	Mace	+2 to all stats, indestructible, resist all 15%, +50% damage, all spell levels -1
Hammer of Jholm	Maul	+4 to 10% damage, indestructable, STR +3, To hit +15%
Civerb's Crudgel	Mace	+35% damage to demons, -5 DEX, -2 MAG
The Celestial Star	Flail	No STR Requirement, +20% light radius, +10 Damage, +8 AC,
Baranar's Star	Morning Star	+12 to hit, +80% damage, +4 VIT, -4 DEX, dura=60, fast attack
Gnarled Root	Club	+20 to hit, +300% damage, +10 DEX, +5 MAG, +10 resist all, -10 armor

Unique Weapon	Type	Attributes/Actions
The Cranium Basher	Maul	+20 pts damage, +15 STR, indestructible, lose all mana, +5% resist all
Schaefer's Hammer	War Hammer	-100% damage, 1 to 50 lightning hit, +50 HP, +30 to hit, resist lightning 80%, +10% light rad
Dreamflange	Mace	+30 MAG, +50 Mana, +50 resist magic, +20% light radius, all spells up 1 level
Staff of Shadows	Long Staff	-10 MAG, +10 to hit, +60% damage, -20% light radius, faster attack
Immolator	Long Staff	Resist fire 20%, fire hit 4 damage, mana +10, -5 VIT
Storm Spire	War Staff	Resist Lightning 50%, Lightning hit 2 to 8, STR +10, MAG -10
Gleamsong	Short Staff	+25 Mana, -3 STR, -3 VIT, 76 charges Phasing Spell
Thundercall	Composite Staff	+35 to hit, lightning hit(1-10), 76 charges Lightning, +30% Resist Lighyning +20% light rad
The Protector	Short Staff	+5 VIT, Attacker takes 1-3 Damage, -5 to damage received, +40 armor, 86 charges of Healing

Unique Weapon	Type	Attributes/Actions
Naj's Puzzler	Long Staff	+20 MAG, +10 DEX, +20% resist all, teleporting 57 charges -25 HP
Mindcry	Quarter Staff (Hvy)	+15 MAG, +15% resist all, all spells up 1 level, 69 charges of Guardian
Rod of Onan	War Staff	50 charges Golem +100% damage, +5 to all stats,
Thinking Cap	Skull Cap	+30 mana, all spells up 2 levels, +20% resist all, durability =1
Helm of Spirits	Helm	gain +5% life per hit
Overlord's Helm	Helm	STR +20, DEX +15, VIT +5, MAG -20, DUR=15,
Fool's Crest	Helm	-4 to all stats, +100 HP, attacker takes 1-3 hp, +1 to 6 damage received per hit
Gotterdamerung	Great Helm	+20 to all stats, +60 armor, all resistance=0%,-4 to damage received, 40% Light Radius
Royal Circlet	Crown	+10 to all stats, + 40 mana, +40 armor, +10% light radius
The Gladiator's Bane	Studded Leather	armor class 25, absorbs 2 hp per hit, durability +200%, all stats -3

Unique Weapon	Type	Attributes/Actions
The Rainbow Cloak	Cloak	Armor Class 10, +1 to all stats, resist all +10%, +5 hp, +50% durability
Wisdom's Wrap	Robe	+5 MAG, +10 mana, +25 resist lightning, Armor = 15, -1 hp per get hit
Leather of Aut	Leather	AC=15, STR +5, MAG -5, Dex +5, indestructable
Sparking Mail	Chain Mail	Armor class 30, attacker gets lightning hit (1-10) in return if it hits
Scavenger Carapace	Breast Plate	-15 hp per get hit, -30 AC, +5 DEX, resist lightning +40%
Nightscape	Cape	Armor class =15, light radius -40%, +20% resist all, faster hit recovery +3 DEX
Naj's Light Plate	Plate Mail	No minimum strength req., +5 MAG, +20 mana, +20% resist all, all spells up 1 level
Demonspike Coat	Full Plate Mail	Armor class= 100, absorbs 6 hp per get hit, +10 STR, indestructible, +50% resist fire
Split Skull Shield	Buckler	+10 to armor, +10 to HP, +2 to STR, -10% light rad, durablity =15
The Deflector	Buckler	AC=7, Resist all 10%,-20% to damage, -5% to hit,

Unique Weapon	Type	Attributes/Actions
Dragon's Breach	Kite Shield	Resist fire 25%, STR +5, AC=20, MAG -5, indestructable
Blackoak Shield	Small Shield	+10 Dex, -10 Vit, armor class 18, -10% light radius, +150% dura
Holy Defender	Large Shield	Armor class 15, absorbs 2 hp per get hit, +20% resist fire, +200% dura, faster block
Stormshield	Tower Shield	Armor class 40, absorbs 4 hp per get hit, +10 STR, indestruct, faster block
Constricting Ring	ring	resist all +75%, wearer constantly loses life
Ring of Engagement	ring	-1 to 2 hp per get hit, attacker takes 1-3 hp (of thorn), adds 5 to AC, damages monster AC
Bramble	ring	-2 to all stats, +3 to damage, +10 mana,
Ring of Regha	ring	MAG +10, Resist magic 10%, +10% light radius, STR -3, DEX -3
The Bleeder	ring	Resist magic 20%, mana +30, HP -10
The Butcher's Cleaver	(quest) Cleaver	+10 STR, 4 to 24 damage, durablilty=10

Unique Weapon	Type	Attributes/Actions
The Undead Crown	(quest) Crown	AC=8, Life Stealing +5%
Empyrean Band	(quest) ring	+2 to all stats, +20% light radius, fast hit recovery, absorbs trap damage
Optic amulet	(quest) amulet	light radius +20%, resist lightning 20%, absorbs 1 damage per hit, MAG +5
Ring of Truth	(quest) ring	+10 HP, absorbs 1 point damage per get hit, resist all 10%,
Harlequin Crest	(quest) Cap	+2 to all stats, +7 HP, +7 Mana, -3 armor, -1 TO DAMAGE RECEIVED
Griswold's Edge	(quest) sword	fire hit 1 to 10, +25 to hit, faster attack, Knocks back monster, mana +20, HP -20
Arkaine's Valor	(quest) Splint Mail	+25 armor class, +10 vit, absorbs 3 pts per hit received, fastest hit recovery
Veil of Steel	(quest) Great Helm	+50%resist all, +60% armor, -30 mana, +15 strength, +15 Vit, -20% light radius

7

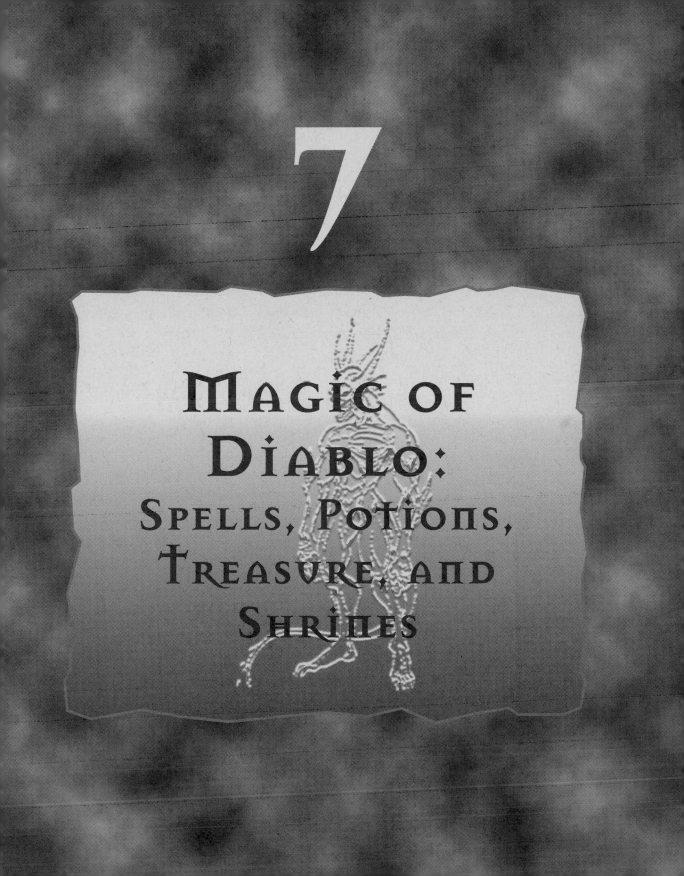

Magic of
Diablo:
Spells, Potions,
Treasure, and
Shrines

One of the most significant aspects of the *Diablo* experience is the tremendous power of magic. Whether brought to bear by a mighty Sorcerer or bestowed at one of the many shrines, the proper understanding and use of the game's many magical components is essential, and quite frequently awesome.

Other chapters in this book deal with magic in the context of combat specific to each monster and situation, but this chapter is devoted purely to the arcane arts as its own subject.

A Magical World

Though this chapter has broad applications in terms of all the character classes, it is foremostly a discussion of Sorcerery, and, as such, applies most directly to Sorcerers.

The fact is that all of the classes learn spells and utilize Mana in slightly different ways, and the class to which magic and Mana matters most is the Sorcerer.

If you experiment with all the classes, you'll find that a Sorcerer's spell levels—and resultant adjustments to Mana economy and damage numbers—increase at a much greater rate than those of a Warrior or Rogue. It is assumed that, as a mage, you're understanding and thus your proper utilization of magic is greater than the other character classes, and you can expect to reap the maximum benefits whenever you employ a spell.

In fact, the Rogue and the Warrior will be constantly finding scrolls and maybe even books that serve no practical purpose as far as they're concerned. Either the item is unusable outright, or the benefits from using it are outweighed by its cash value.

For the Sorcerer, however, magic is the meat and potatoes of the *Diablo* experience. Or perhaps the smoke and mirrors. Herein lies the complete list of spells, and some tactical considerations for each. Again, it's possible to extrapolate this information for any of the classes, but a spell recommended here as a devastating offensive

TIP

READING MATERIAL

IF YOU'RE PLAYING THE WARRIOR OR ROGUE, TREAT MAGICAL BOOKS JUST AS YOU WOULD EQUIP ANY OTHER ITEM. IF IT'S A SPELL YOU DON'T HAVE, AND WOULD LIKE, READ AWAY. IF, ON THE OTHER HAND, IT'S A SPELL YOU ALREADY HAVE, OR PERHAPS ONE THAT COSTS SO MUCH MANA THAT CASTING IT BECOMES A BURDEN, YOU MIGHT WANT TO CONSIDER SELLING THE BOOK. SIMPLY SAVE YOUR GAME BEFORE YOU READ, AND CHECK THE RESULTANT MANA COST AND DAMAGE NUMBERS. IF THE SPELL DOESN'T SUIT YOUR NEEDS, HOCK THE BOOK.

The Apocalypse Spell is one of the most devastating to virtually all the creatures in the labyrinth.

weapon might fall somewhat short of that evaluation when cast by a Warrior or Rogue. Remember, generally speaking, that a spell lasts longer and does more damage as it increases in levels.

THE SPELLS

With the lone exception of the Holy Bolt Spell, magic in *Diablo* falls into three categories: Fire, Lightning, and Transformational Conjurations (General Magic). There are also two multiplayer spells in the game, which allow one character to assist another through magic.

Holy Bolt

This spell is an intense, fast shot of Holy magic that harms only the undead with one horrible, dark master of an exception. If there is one spell you can depend on in the endgame, this is it. Cherish every book of Holy Bolt. It's a great spell to use in multiplayer situations, because a miss won't hurt your comrades.

Fire Spells

A broad range of Fire-based magic means a wide array of tactical considerations. A few things to consider, where each spell is concerned.

Firebolt

This is your basic, all-purpose beginner spell. Every Sorcerer gets one, and it works well enough, shooting a smallish fireball at your opponents. On the first few levels, this spell works great and doesn't cost much Mana. To really get the most from the Firebolt Spell, you must acquire, and read, several books.

Inferno

The Inferno spell is the *Diablo* equivalent of a flame-thrower. Casting this spell produces a single, focused stream of flame, albeit only for a short distance at the beginner levels. The heat of the Inferno Spell is more intense than that of the Firebolt, and the effect lingers longer and longer as your level of experience rises. At the highest levels, this spell is one of the best, devastating in effect and relatively easy on Mana.

WALL OF FIRE

This is a very useful spell. As you might guess, it throws a wall of flames across whatever space you're in, wasting anything in its path and blocking the path of many others. It's possible to compress the Firewall in a doorway, and thus cause it to get rid of any holes in the wall of flames. Also, notice that some monsters, especially animals, fear fire. If you have a ranged attack, a Fire Wall can hold those monsters at bay while you switch to some other method of destruction.

FLAME WAVE

The Flame Wave Spell is akin to the Wall of Fire, but it actually sweeps the room from one end to the other when cast. As a result, this is perhaps more of an offensive spell than the Wall, since it spreads and dissipates in a matter of seconds, and can't be used to block a door. If you have a goodly supply of Mana, casting several Flame Waves in rapid succession can be an incredibly easy way to clear a large room.

FIREBALL

The Fireball Spell packs a tremendous amount of fire energy into a small projectile, which strikes for significant damage and then erupts into a burning cloud which also inflicts damage. Mana hungry, this is one of those you should save for foes that really warrant the harshest treatment. It should be noted that the fireball shoots faster as the level of spell increases.

GUARDIAN

The Guardian Spell, which all players learn in the Chamber of Bone, invokes a three-headed dragon which spouts fire at any monster currently within range. The dragon is fixed in place, so you have to remain in the general area or lure creatures to it once the spell is cast in order for it to target nearby foes.

Elemental

The Elemental Spell is one of the coolest, and most effective, in the game. If a monster hates fire magic, it's gonna downright loath seeing the Elemental headed his way. When the spell is cast, a fire elemental appears in front of you, and goes charging off towards the target. Even if a target is out of your sight, the Elemental will attack if it finds the ememy. When he hits home, the Elemental erupts as a Fireball Spell.

Apocalypse (Scroll & Staff Only)

The high-end of the Fire Spells, Apocalypse lives up to its name. This spell is made to cast while standing in large, angry packs of monsters, a frequent occurrence once you've ventured a ways into the dungeon. Most of the monsters in the vicinity simply blow up, while all are significantly weakened. Buy the scroll whenever the Witch has one, and hoard any you happen to find. It's worth boosting your magical powers just to read this scroll, especially when you're thinning out the crowds on level 16 before facing Diablo.

Lightning

Lightning-based spells tend to have a somewhat broader application in Diablo than the fire-based spells, just because of a their inherent range, which is effectively limitless. Early in the game, when the choice is between Firebolt or Lightning Bolt, only Lightning-resistant monsters get the hotfoot. Note that the higher the level of spell, the longer the Lightning Bolt becomes.

CHARGED BOLT

This spell produces multiple Lightning Projectiles, which bounce off the walls until they strike a foe or eventually dissipate. Firing it several times into a relatively small, enclosed space can have devastating effects, especially on the lesser monsters early in the game.

Chain Lightning is a powerful weapon that sends out more bolts as your level increases.

Lightning

One step up from the Charged Bolt, this spells allows you to send a concentrated stream of electricity at one target. Again, rapid firing is great for thinning crowds.

Flash

The Flash Spell deals an insane amount of damage at very close range: A kind of panic-button spell. Notice that though the energy ripples around your entire body, you still have to select an individual target to take the brunt of the attack, just as you would target any other spell. Nearby monsters will all take radius damage, but you need to select a primary target.

Chain Lightning

A bigger, badder Lightning Spell, Mana-hungry but worth it when you're fighting numerous monsters that have a resistance to Fire.

Nova (Scroll & Staff Only)

The Nova Spell functions like a devastating radial Lightning attack. It's so powerful, in fact, that even a Sorcerer cannot learn it from a book.

Transformational Conjurations

Aside from Fire and Lightning, the rest of the spells, with multiplayer exceptions noted, can be lumped under Transformational Conjurations (a.k.a.—General Magic).

IDENTIFY (SCROLL & STAFF ONLY)

This important spell determines the nature of magical objects: Not all magical items assist your persona, and some may even cause you harm. Adria generally has a Scroll of Identify in her inventory, and you should buy them whenever they appear. That way, when you're down in the dungeon, you don't have to go back to Tristram to find out if an item is worth equipping.

The Town Portal Spell gives you a way back to the surface to gather more resources.

TOWN PORTAL

Always available in scroll form from Adria the Witch, the Town Portal is the primary means of travel between the dungeon and Tristram. Sure, there are several stairways. None of them ever seems to be right beside you, terminating a few yards from the center of town, when you need it. Town Portal is. If you should start to amass extra scrolls, throw them on the ground in Tristram near where the portal opens. When you emerge, pick one up as a matter of habit. That's a great way to be sure you can always get back to town, even if all your Mana has been expended.

STONE CURSE

A devastating spell, best for fighting those nasty Uniques. You need to be relatively close by when you cast Stone Curse, since it's only temporary, and you don't want to waste spell time running over to your adversary. Once stoned, a few whacks with any weapon on hand is usually all it takes to reduce the dark ones to rubble.

HEALING

The Healing Spell is a welcome addition to your repertoire, though it really depends on the character class as to how and when you use it. For a Sorcerer, burning Mana during combat to heal is not the best option, especially if you've been doing a good job of stock-piling those Scrolls of Healing from Pepin and Adria. Remember, you can hotkey a scroll just as you would a spell in your Spellbook, and it won't cost Mana to use it. Generally, it's best to go that route, and heal with Mana when you're not in the heat of battle.

RESURRECT (MULTIPLAYER SCROLL & STAFF ONLY)

Just in case, Pepin always has a Resurrect scroll in his inventory during multiplayer games. One word of caution: Using the spell only gives the raised character one Hit Point, so don't do it in hostile territory unless you're prepared to cast . . .

HEAL OTHER (MULTIPLAYER ONLY)

The Heal Other spell allows you to aid a weary comrade in multiplayer games—Simply highlight your "target" to see their hit points and right click them back to health.

TELEKINESIS

This spell allows the caster to manipulate distant objects with the power of the mind, opening chests, Sarcophogi pushing monsters back, and doors.

INFRAVISION (SCROLL ONLY)

The Infravision spell allows the caster to see through walls, displaying lurking monsters in a reddish hue. Seldom is it a significant tactical advantage, unless you're lining up a Wall of Fire. For grins, try using Infravision outside the Chamber of Bone's main room.

PHASE

The Phase spell teleports the caster in a random direction. Trying to teleport from one area into another very specific area with this spell is tedious at best and recklessly Mana-hungry at worst. Instead, use this spell to leap from one section of dungeon to another, when you realize you have to make a long, elliptical backtrack or if your being swarmed by attackers.

MANA SHIELD

Probably the most significant spell in the game from a Sorcerer's standpoint, Mana Shield allows the caster to utilize Mana points as Hit Points, drawing off of Mana instead of health when damage is sustained in combat. For the Sorcerer, which usually has a huge Mana

The Mana Shield can save your life at the lower levels—literally—especially if you are a Sorcerer.

point total and a puny bit of Health, the effect can quite literally be the difference between life and death. Buy a Scroll of Mana Shield whenever you possibly can from Adria, and save them up for when the dungeon gets really hostile. The spell wears off when you move between levels or trip back to town, so unless you have the spell you can never have too many scrolls.

GOLEM

The Golem spell is an amusing bit of magic that invokes a large Golem in your defense. The monster follows you around in a kind of

The Golem Spell gives you a helper who'll
seek out your enemies and destroy them.

general way—and for a goodly duration—throttling any monster it can get its big stone hands on. The Golem is particularly effective against advocates, as it is immune to their Flash Spell. A Golem's hit points are based on the character's Mana & Spell level, and when a second Golem is summoned, the old one is replaced with the new.

BONE SPIRIT AND BLOOD STAR

The highest-level spells in the game are those which actually effect the characteristics of a monster aside from its health. By employing these spells properly, you can effectively reduce a significant monster to a shadow of its former self. But be prepared, these Monster Class spells demand you to sacrifice Health as well as Mana when cast.

BONE SPIRIT

The Bone Spirit spell reduces a target's Hit Points by a third every time it strikes. After two or three shots, even the (formerly) toughest foe can be taken out with one quick follow-up.

BLOOD STAR

The Blood Star Spell whips any monster without Magic resistance. Instead of doing a range of damage, a hit with Blood Star reduces a foe's hit point by one thrid of the caster's magic characteristic number.

SPELL INDEX

The following section lays out *Diablo*'s spells, providing the minimum Magic and Mana levels each spell requires for execution; the level where you're most likely to find it; the extra effects that accumulate with each book you add to your inventory; the number of charges available with each spellcasting staff; and each spell's cost in gold.

TABLE 7-1. SPELLS

Spell	Min. Magic (book/staff, scroll)	Mana	Extra Book Effects
Firebolt	0, 0	6	+1 Damage, +2 Speed, −5 Mana
Charged Bolt	25, 0	6	+1 bolt per two levels
Holy Bolt	20, 0	7	+2 Speed, −1 Mana
Healing	17, 0	(level x2)+5	+6 Healing, −3 Mana
Heal Other	17, 0	(level x2)+5	+6 Healing, −3 Mana
Lightning	20, 0	12	bolt longer per 2 levels, −1 Mana
Identify	23, 0	n/a	n/a
Resurrect	30, 0	20	gives 10 Hit Points to resurrected
Wall of Fire	27, 17	2/3 current level	lasts 5% longer, −2 Mana
Telekinesis	33, 21	15	−2 Mana
Inferno	20, 19	11	1/2 current level% Damage, −1 Mana

To determine the Damage a spell does, simply refer to the Spell-book. Each spell's damage is the result of a unique computation which considers your Magic characteristic number, the level of the spell, and the level of the caster. Of course, the actual damage you do depends on the monster you attack, and considers not only that monsters physical defenses but also any magical resistances or immunities.

Level (scroll, staff, book)	Cost (scroll, book)	Staff Charges
n/a, 1, 1	50, 100	40–80
n/a, 1, 1	50, 1,000	40–80
n/a, 1, 1	50, 1,000	40–80
1, 1, 1	50, 1,000	20–40
1, 1, 1	50, 1,000	20–40
2, 3, 4	150, 3,000	20–60
1, n/a, n/a	100, n/a	n/a
1, n/a, n/a	250, n/a	n/a
2, 2, 3	400, 6,000	8–16
n/a, 2, 2	200, 1,500	20–40
1, 2, 3	100, 2,000	20–40

Spell	Min. Magic (book/staff, scroll)	Mana	Extra Book Effects
Town Portal	20, 0	35	−3 Mana
Flash	33, 21	30	+10% Damage, −2 Mana
Infravision	36, 23	40	lasts 15% longer, −5 Mana
Phase	39, 25	12	−2 Mana
Mana Shield	25, 0	33	−3% to damage taken (max 21%)
Flame Wave	45, 29	35	+1 wave square, −3 Mana
Fireball	48, 31	16	double, +2 Speed, −1 Mana
Stone Curse	51, 33	60	lasts 15% longer, −3 Mana
Chain Lightning	54, 35	30	−1 Mana
Guardian	61, 47	50	+10% Damage, 1−second duration, −2 Mana
Elemental	68, 53	23	+10% Damage, −2 Mana
Nova	87, 57	60	+10% Damage, −3 Mana
Golem	81, 51	80	−4 Mana
Teleport	105, 81	35	−3 Mana
Apocalypse	149, 117	150	−6 Mana
Bone Spirit	34, n/a	24	−1 Mana
Blood Star	70, 46	25	+3 Damage, −2 Mana

Level (scroll, staff, book)	Cost (scroll, book)	Staff Charges
2, 3, 3	200, 300	8–12
3, 4, 5	500, 1,500	20–40
4, n/a, n/a	600 n/a	n/a
3, 6, 7	200, 3,500	40–80
4, 5, 6	1,200, 1,600	4–10
5, 8, 9	650, 1,000	20–40
4, 7, 8	300, 8,000	40–80
3, 5, 6	800, 12,000	8–16
5, 7, 8	750, 11,000	20–60
—	950, 14,000	16–32
4, 6, 8	700, 10,500	20–60
7, 10, n/a	1,300, n/a	16–32
5, 9, 11	100, 18,000	16–32
7, 12, 14	1,250, 20,000	16–32
11, 15, n/a	2,000, n/a	8–12
7, 7, 9	800, 11,500	20–60
10, 13, 14	1,800, 27,500	20–60

MAGICAL POTIONS

With the exception of unique quest-specific Elixirs, there are only a handful of potions in all of Tristram and the dungeon below. The vast majority of potions, which can be purchased either from the Healer or the Witch, concern the process of healing oneself or restoring Mana. Understanding their proper use is a matter of simple economics—both of the gold in your pocket and the space in your inventory—and class considerations.

REPLENISHING HEALTH AND MANA:

WARRIOR AND SORCERER

The difference in how each class best utilizes potions of Health and Mana lies in the simple understanding that a Warrior and a Sorcerer, at the highest levels of experience, have drastically different totals in a full tank of either.

The Warrior, of course, has 300 or so Hit Points and perhaps 150 of Mana, while the Sorcerer's are virtually reversed.

This extreme example serves well to illustrate a situation that is general to the Warrior and Sorcerer. You Rogues get off lucky in this regard, as your Health and Mana tend to be of equal amounts. More on that to follow.

For the Warrior and Sorcerer to consider the two aspects of economy—gold and space—there is a simple equation: The most economical potion in terms of space is the Potion of Full Rejuvenation. One potion, full meters.

The problem is, those little gold beauties are 600 Gold a pop.

For arguments sake, assume that a potion of Partial Health and a Potion of Partial Mana do the same amount of replenishing to their respective traits. It's actually a range of replenishing, but it's relatively the same.

So if you're a Warrior, why wouldn't you buy Full Potions of Healing, and Partial Potions of Mana? For a total of 200 Gold, you're getting virtually the same effect as a Potion of Full Rejuvenation. No, those meters might not be *entirely* full. But your pockets are fuller with Gold.

The Sorcerer's situation is analogous: Consider Buying Full Mana and Partial Healing. The consideration is made more drastic for the Sorcerer due to the fact that the Healing spell is actually Mana-efficient for him at some point. The Sorcerer is more likely than a Warrior to have 30 or 40 Mana Points in the meter after a fight: Why not cast Healing before using a Potion of Full Mana? If that and a Potion of Partial Healing don't get you up to full meters . . . it must have been a hell of a fight.

The Rogue

The Rogue tends to fall in the middle of the pack, which means that there are pros and cons to any scheme you might develop for replenishing Health and Mana.

No matter what class you're playing, the point is that those Potions of Full Rejuvenation are a bad investment. Don't go out of your way to buy them.

As a Rogue, either your Health and Mana will be relatively equal, or a skew will be the result of magical items you choose to equip. Basically, you have to look at your stats, and judge which of the above situations—the Warrior's or the Sorcerer's—is more analogous to the present condition of your characteristics.

Realize that changing your equipment drastically may alter the most efficient way to replenish your resources, and always keep a good cross-section of potions on hand, especially if there's a chance you might be changing equipment down in the dungeon.

THE ELIXIRS

Once you've descended into the Hell levels of the dungeon, both Adria and Pepin begin to carry a random generation of Elixirs in their items for sale.

For a cost of 5,000 Gold each, you can buy an Elixir that increases your stats one point in either Strength, Magic, or Dexterity. Potions of Vitality do show up from time to time, but they are much rarer.

Usually, the temptation is to burn any large chunk of Gold you might get from selling high-end treasure on these Elixirs. Up until the very end of the game, however, that can be a bad idea.

In the last two levels of the dungeon await some of the very best treasure, and the best of the best requires the highest skill characteristics to use.

Instead of blowing 20,000 Gold with a level of dungeon left to play (and Diablo's level, 16, is a level to remember) hang onto that Gold. You may need to boost a crucial category one or two points in order to use the best item in the game—and already having spent the Gold on the wrong type of Elixir makes Diablo laugh and laugh. . . .

MAGICAL TREASURE:

UNIQUE RINGS AND AMULETS

Among the magical jewelry and tonics you'll find in your travels, a few are very special:

- **The Constricting Ring:** This item increases your overall resistance by 75%, but you'll consistently lose life while wearing it. You'll find it on Level 5.

- **The Ring of Engagement.** This item decreases your Hit Points per strike by 1–2, your attackers take 1–3 Hit Points damage, it adds 5 to your Armor Class, and damages the Monster's Armor Class. It freezes nearby monsters in their tracks. You'll find it on Level 11.

- **The Ring of Truth:** This item absorbs one Hit Point per strike received, and adds +10 to your overall resistance and Hit Points. Complete the Poison Water Quest to acquire this ring.

- **The Empyrean Band:** This item improves all your stats by +2, improves your ability to see in the dark by +20%, absorbs trap damage, and improves hit recovery quickly. Complete the Magic Rock quest to acquire this ring.

- **The Optic Amulet:** This item increases your ability to see in the dark by 20%, adds +5 to Magic, increases your resistance to lightning by 20%, and absorbs 1 Hit Point each time you take a blow. Complete the Halls of the Blind quest to find it.

PROPERTIES OF MAGICAL SHRINES

Shrines provide another of *Diablo*'s intriguing aspects.

Most of the time a shrine, which activates when you step up to it, offers only a cryptic clue to its function. The hint is often lost on the weary adventurer. Here, then, is a complete list of shrine types, the message each bestows, and its effect. Now you can highlight a shrine, determine its type, and refer to the following table to decide whether to activate it. Sometimes, as in the case of the Cryptic Shrine, the Thaumaturgic Shrine, or the Spiritual Shrine, it clearly behooves you to prepare before triggering the effect. . . .

TABLE 7-2. SHRINES

Shrine	Effect
Mysterious	Adds 5 points to one random stat, takes 1 point from others.
Hidden	Adds 10 points to the maximum and current durability to all items, −10 to one.
Gloomy	Add +2AC to all shields, helmets, armor. −1 to all weapons max damage.
Weird	Adds +1 to all weapons max damage
Magical	Casts Mana shield on the player
Stone	Recharges all staves
Religious	"heals" all weapon durability
Enchanted	One spell down a level, all others up one level.
Thaumaturgic	All chests on the level regenerate with new items
Fascinating	Gives you Firebolt +2, but you lose 1/10 of your maximum Mana.
Cryptic	fills Mana ball casts nova spell from player
Eldritch	Health and Mana potions become rejuvenation
Eerie	Adds 2 points to your magic.
Divine	Kicks out either 2 full rejuvenation potions or 1 full Mana & 1 full healing, and fills Mana and life balls
Holy	Teleports you to another place on the level.

Message

"Some are weakened as one grows strong"

"New strength is forged through destruction"

"Those who defend seldom attack."

"The sword of justice is swift and sharp."

"While the spirit is vigilant the body thrives"

"The powers of Mana refocused renews"

"Time cannot diminish the power of steel"

"Magic is not always what it seems to be."

"What once was opened now is closed"

"Intensity comes at the cost of wisdom"

"Arcane power brings destruction"

"crimson and azure become as the sun"

"Knowledge & Wisdom at the cost of self"

"Drink and be refreshed"

"Wherever you go, there you are"

Shrine	Effect
Sacred	Charged bolt +2 levels, lose 1/10 max Mana
Spiritual	Fills your inventory with gold.
Spooky	full rejuv. Potions for other players
Abandoned	Add +2 to Dex
Creepy	Add +2 to STR
Quiet	Add +2 to VIT
Secluded	Completes automap for current level
Ornate	Holy Bolt level +2, lose 1/10 max Mana
Glimmering	All items are identified
Tainted	All other players get +1–3 random stats, −1 to other.

Message

"Energy comes at the cost of wisdom"

"Riches abound when least expected"

You: "where avarice fails, patience gains reward"
Others: "Blessed by a benevolent companion"

"The hands of men may be guided by fate"

"Strength is bolstered by heavenly faith"

"The essence of life flows from within"

"The way is cleared when viewed from above"

"Salvation comes at the cost of wisdom"

"Mysteries revealed in the light of reason"

You: "Those who are last may yet be first"
Others: "Generosity brings its own rewards"

8

THE QUESTS

T he object of this game, of course, is to make it all the way to the deepest, darkest dungeon level and kill Satan himself. Along the way, however, you'll be invited to complete a random assortment of ancillary missions called *quests*. Some are essential to completing the game, and all are worth the excursion, at the very least for the experience you gain. Often, of course, you'll receive some Unique and valuable item as reward for fulfilling a quest.

The smell of death surrounds me.

Diablo's quests include three subtypes—external set pieces, internal set pieces, and contained quests. To a certain extent, all these side missions are random; "The Butcher," for example, will always be there on Level 2, but never in the same place.

External set pieces take place on special dungeon levels, roughly half the size of a normal level, to which you gain access after receiving information from one of the townspeople or from a book you find in the dungeon. The set-piece levels themselves are static, so once you're there you get the same puzzle every time. These include "The Curse of King Leoric;" "Poisoned Water Supply;" "The Chamber of Bone," and "Archbishop Lazarus."

Internal set pieces involve special rooms set within a randomly generated dungeon level. The rooms themselves remain the same, although their locations change with each game. These include "The Butcher;" "Ogden's Sign;" "Armor of Valor;" "The Halls of the Blind;" "The Anvil of Fury," and "The Warlord of Blood."

Contained quests are special ventures requiring no special locations. These include "The Black Mushroom;" "Gharbad the Weak;" "Zhar the Mad," and "Lachdanan."

QUEST GROUPING

As you begin each new game of *Diablo*, the computer chooses from among all possible quests, predetermining which you'll find as the game progresses. Far from just taking a random sampling of a single list, however, the game breaks the quests into subsets based on difficulty, and then chooses a random sampling from those smaller groups.

Some quests are always included (mostly as the game begins and also near its conclusion). The following quest summaries note this information parenthetically for each. Table 8-1 shows the grouping the computer selects from to determine any one game's overall content.

TABLE 8-1. QUEST GROUPS

Group 1 (1 of 2)	King Leoric's Curse or Poison Water
Group 2 (2 of 3)	The Butcher, Ogden's Sign, Gharbad the Weak
Group 3 (2 of 3)	The Magic Rock, Armor of Valor, Halls of the Blind
Group 4 (2 of 3)	Zhar the Mad, The Black Mushroom, The Anvil of Fury
Group 5 (1 of 2)	The Warlord of Blood, Lachdanan

Aside from quests selected from these groupings, a single-player game always includes "The Chamber of Bone," "Archbishop Lazarus," "King Leorics's Curse," and, of course, the final showdown with Diablo. It's worth noting that in Battle.net, the quests featuring the Butcher, the Vile Betrayer, and Diablo are present, as well, though as part of the regular dungeon levels, without the ancillary set pieces the single-player game features.

Beware of the fires of hell.

Quest Summaries and Solutions

You might not believe it the first time "The Butcher" kicks your butt, but the computer tailors *Diablo*'s quests nicely to your character's relative experience level. Most often, a quest involves battling one or more Unique monsters, either to claim an item off its corpse or to trade any treasure thus garnered for something more valuable.

Sometimes completing the quest is just that straightforward: Search and destroy. A few tactical insights, however, can go a long way toward smoothing out the rough spots. Consider the type of dungeon level you're fighting on, and don't forget to highlight any Unique and check the Dialogue Box to remind yourself of a particular foe's magical defenses.

THE BUTCHER (GROUP 2: LEVEL 2)

Trigger Character: The Wounded Townsman at the church entrance

As you approach the desecrated cathedral for the first time, you encounter a dying man. "Please, master," he says. "Listen to me. The Archbishop Lazarus, he led us down here to find the lost prince. The bastard led us into a trap! Now everyone is dead . . . killed by a demon he called the Butcher. Avenge us! Find the Butcher and slay him so that our souls may finally rest. . . ."

Two-thirds of the time, this is the first quest you encounter in *Diablo*, though you'll note that it's actually culled from the second set in terms of computer randomization. What that means, in practical terms, is that you may not be ready for the Butcher the first time you encounter him, on Level 2.

Actually, you're ready for him the first time you pick up a Short Bow.

The Butcher, as Adria the Witch tells you, "is a sadistic creature that delights in the torture and pain of others." He wields a huge Cleaver, with which he dismembers his opponents. Often, a Warrior

The Butcher is a serious threat to beginning adventurers . . . Beware!

can live through a couple of Cleaver swipes, but early in the game the Sorcerer or Rogue tends to lose limbs at an alarming rate.

You'll find the Butcher in a large room on Level 2. Make sure you clear the dungeon level in its entirety before opening the Butcher's room: He'll rush outside to greet you, and you don't want any other traffic in the neighborhood while you make his acquaintance.

The simplest trick to humbling the fiend lies in the structure of the dungeon level itself. As you've probably noticed, there are several junctures in the level where steel grating flanking a doorway allows you to see (or shoot) into a room before opening the door.

Yes, that's right: The Butcher's only major tactical deficiency is his inability to open doors. After clearing out the level, simply find such a grating-flanked doorway (unobstructed by fallen monsters). Let the Butcher chase you to that point, and close the door in his face. Equip a bow. Fire at will.

This may take awhile if you're playing a character other than the Rogue, because a low-level character in the other classes is unlikely to have much bow proficiency. But anyone can hit the broad side of a demon from point-blank range, and it's worth plucking the bow string a few times to kill the Butcher without expending any Health or Mana.

When the Butcher completes his imitation of a large, angry porcupine, you'll lay hands on the Butcher's Cleaver. For the next couple of levels, that will kill most monsters with a single swipe. Sooner or later (probably sooner if you're playing the Sorcerer or Rogue), you'll want to unload the axe and purchase something a little more suited to your class.

POISONED WATER SUPPLY (GROUP I: LEVEL 2)

Trigger Character: Pepin the Healer

This quest begins when Pepin the Healer seeks your help in stopping a sickness running through the town. Its source is a fouled water supply. The problem lies in a nasty demon infestation on Level 2: The presence of evil taints an underground spring.

Down on Level 2 you'll find an obvious entrance, "To A Dark Pas-

sage"—a crack in the wall surrounded by an array of elements usually reserved for important tomes of lore. Beyond the crack lies a set-piece level of caverns. Prepare for combat on arrival: A small band of fallen ones await you.

Traverse the few rock corridors and dispose of the Goat Demons and lesser beasts. When you've dropped the last of the level's monsters, you'll hear a trumpet of triumph in the distance, and the fouled waterway will clear to blue before your eyes.

Return to Pepin. He'll give you the Ring of Truth, a Unique Item that will serve you well early in the game, and perhaps even deep into the dungeon.

The Curse of King Leoric (Group 1: Level 3)

Trigger Character: Ogden the Tavern Owner

This quest begins when Ogden the Tavern Owner solicits your help. He'll tell you the story of King Leoric who, years ago, lost his son to kidnappers. Grief drove Leoric mad, forcing his knights and priest to destroy him. Upon his death, he cursed the town and his former followers. Now, risen from the dead, he rules a legion of undead minions within the labyrinth.

"Please, good master," Ogden implores you, "Put his soul at ease by destroying his now-cursed form."

Plan on expending some serious Health and Mana resources to finish off Leoric. You'll be fighting in cramped quarters with a bunch of enemies, and there's just no way for a low-level character not to

*Don't forget about the Holy Bolt Spell
when facing Leoric and his minions.*

take some damage. Refresh yourself before you go looking for trouble, and bring a club or axe, the better to smash Skeletons with.

Go to Level 3 and locate an obvious passage to Leoric's Tomb. Enter and find yourself on a small level, just stuffed with Skeletons. In fact, Leoric produces the monsters as you watch. Put him out of business as quickly as you can, lest he create an insurmountable horde of bonemen.

As reward for Leoric's demise, you'll receive the Skeleton Crown, another Unique Item that drops when the king dies. Again, although

the Crown's decent enhancements will help any character type through the next few dungeon levels, you'll want to sell it when an upgrade becomes available that better suits your character's specific needs.

Also, notice that there is a secret antechamber to King Leoric's Tomb (aside from the small room with the obvious treasure chests). To access the hidden area, destroy each of the crucified Skeletons in the large room's corners. When the last falls to the ground, a door opens in the middle of the long northern wall. Inside waits more foes and treasures.

OGDEN'S SIGN (GROUP 2: LEVEL 4)

Trigger Character: Ogden the Tavern Owner

Those demons have stolen the sign to Ogden's Rising Sun Inn and Tavern, and it's up to you to get it back. Cain the Storyteller thinks the demons may deem the sign sacred and powerful, like the sun, which they fear. Adria the Witch warns you not to let seemingly bizarre demon behavior fool you. "No mortal can truly understand the mind of a demon," she says. "Never let their erratic actions confuse you, as that, too, may be their plan."

In fact, you must claim the sign before a disgusting little creature named Snotspill will let you advance from the fourth to the fifth dungeon level. Snotspill waits in a set piece on Level 4, between you and the staircase to Level 5. You must acquire the sign to open the way to the down staircase, although you have two options thereafter.

*Snotspill and his friends believe the Tavern
sign gives them great power.*

For starters, the sign is in the large chest in the same small set-piece area as Snotspill. Several massive monsters stand between you and the prize. With the sign in your possession, you can either hand it over to Snotspill (of course, no self-respecting adventurer would do that), or you can return it to Ogden.

If you give the sign to Snotspill, he'll thank you and then you'll have to kill him for some random item. If you take the sign back to Ogden, he'll rummage around and produce the Harlequin Crest as

your reward. The Crest is a decent little cap, relative to the other items you'll have access to at that point in the game.

When you return to Snotspill's area after giving Ogden the sign, a massive attack of Fallen Ones ensues. Although there are a ton of them, they'll all panic and flee briefly as long as you can keep killing them. Target the closest monster and attack. Rinse and repeat.

Yes, Snotspill will drop a Magic item when he dies, usually a decent weapon of some sort.

GHARBAD THE WEAK (GROUP 2: LEVEL 4)

Trigger Character: Gharbad, a groveling Flesh Clan Demon

The first time you find him, Gharbad whines and pleads for his life, promising that, if you let him live, he'll do you a favor in return. The second time you meet him, he swears that "something for you I am making;" he even gives you a token of good faith.

When you see him the third time, he's still full of promises, and he's almost done with the project.

On your fourth encounter, Gharbad decides his project is too good for you, and attacks.

It's a decent confrontation but an entirely reasonable proposition for you by the time you meet up with him. When you rid the world of this whiny piece of dungeon debris, he'll drop a formidable Mace you can add to your inventory. There's no real trick to Gharbad's demise; he's a midrange Unique in almost every regard, and as such serves as

*Gharbad the Weak: He's a real shiner,
but don't turn your back on him.*

a good barometer of your skills. Prepare to heal yourself in battle, and dispose of "the Weak" as you see fit.

THE MAGIC ROCK (GROUP 3: LEVEL 5)

Trigger Character: Griswold the Blacksmith

Griswold tells you about a "sky rock" a caravan brought into the area. Cloaked riders attacked the caravan and stole the rock, which the

Blacksmith now covets. If you could only lay hands on the prize he could make something useful, he promises.

Down on Level 5, in no particular place, you'll find the rock sitting on a small table. If you take it to Griswold, he breaks the rock into smaller stones and sets them in the Empyrean Band. Unless you're tripping over magical rings every time you turn around, the Band's broad positive effects will make it a mainstay for much of the remaining game.

ARMOR OF VALOR (GROUP 3: LEVEL 5)

Trigger Object: The Book of Blood

When you find the Book of Blood, pass through the Book's room and into the next to locate the Altar of Blood. The first of the Blood Stones should be on the ground nearby. Plug it into the Altar. Now look at the map: A doorway has appeared in the wall of the set-piece, very near where you stand. In that room some Horned Demons and another Blood Stone await you. The Stone, when set in the pedestal, opens a similar room on the opposite side of the set-piece.

When you've set all three Blood Stones in the Altar of Blood, a final chamber opens, and you'll battle yet more Horned Demons for the ultimate prize—Arkaine's Valor. The armor of the hero Arkaine is simply the best you can hope to acquire early in the game, regardless of class. Through the next five levels of dungeon, it's highly unlikely you'll come across anything better.

THE CHAMBER OF BONE (ALWAYS INCLUDED)

Trigger Object: A book

A mysterious book you find on Level 6 opens the way to a secret staircase, leading to the Chamber of Bone. They don't call it that for nothing.

The Chamber is a small separate level, with two broad hallways flanking a central chamber. At the end of each hall lie two large

The Skeleton Lever unlocks the Chamber of Bone.

switches. Horned Demons, Unseen, and the occasional Skeleton stand guard. Those switches open two small ancillary rooms, featuring more Skeletons and two chests stuffed with prime treasures.

Before you open the door to the central chamber, prepare to break some bones. The room is stuffed with Skeletons, and it behooves you to keep them from escaping, if at all possible. Target the doorway, and cut loose. If you're playing the Warrior, you've got a lot of serious whacking in store. Whatever class you play, a couple of Firewall Spells can go a long way to evening the odds.

When the chamber finally falls silent, pass through into the larger area (prepare for a few more Horned Demons and Unseen). When the last monster succumbs, read the nearby book to acquire the Guardian Spell, a handy three-headed fire monster that spouts from the ground to hurl flaming orbs at any enemy currently attacking within range.

THE HALLS OF THE BLIND (GROUP 3: LEVEL 7)

Trigger Object: The Book of the Blind

The Dark Book foretells of the Halls of the Blind in a book you find, opening doorways to a set piece from hell.

You'll probably come across the Halls of the Blind before you can actually enter them—a large, figure eight–shaped hall around two small rooms. Once you've read the book, two doorways open on either side of the structure, allowing you to peek into a seemingly empty area.

Of course, the area is far from empty. It is, in fact, crawling with diabolical Illusion Weavers. If you stand up in the doorway, the monsters won't be able to pass into the hall to surround you. That's the key to fighting any monster of this type—realizing they don't teleport or etherealize, but simply turn invisible. Thus you can jam them up at junctures, and even attack them, while they're invisible. So, if you're packing a bow or some decent magic, you don't even have to wait for them to show up in front of you. Cut loose into the empty room, and bodies will drop.

Expect more Weavers in the small central rooms (clear the halls before opening the doors). In one of the rooms you'll lay hands on the Optic Amulet.

ZHAR THE MAD (GROUP 4: LEVEL 8)

Trigger Character: Zhar

You'll find Zhar busy with his thoughts in a library. The first time you meet him, he'll lay a Spellbook on you and tell you to get lost.

If you don't take the hint, or if you attempt to pilfer his bookshelf, Zhar attacks. As Uniques go, Zhar can be bad news. He lobs Fireballs—probably your first opportunity to experience that spell. To make matters worse, Zhar won't give chase; he prefers instead to guard his books and lob fire at you whenever you peek into the room.

Obviously, you must trot out some big guns for this guy. If you're playing the Warrior, expect Zhar to teleport when you run over to attack him. Watch the floor when he disappears: You can judge by the

lit section where he's going, and where he'll re-materialize. Anticipate his arrival with the worst of intentions.

If you've got a decent ranged attack, by all means use it. Regardless of your offensive tactics, prepare to heal yourself, and equip anything you own that has a hint of resistance to fire.

THE BLACK MUSHROOM (GROUP 4: LEVEL 9)

Trigger Object: The Fungal Tome

This is one of the game's most convoluted quests, but the payoff is worth it, and it really requires no more than a couple of extra trips to town to get the job done.

Down on Level 9, encountering the Fungal Tome signals the beginning of the quest. Take it to the Witch, who tells you now she needs only a large Black Mushroom to complete a concoction she's brewing.

(You may have run across the mushroom patch already down on Level 9. It looks like a small area of incongruous texture on the dungeon floor. When you click on it you understand it's not yet usable.)

Give the Fungal Tome to the Witch and return to the mushroom patch to search. Out pops one big (bloated, disgusting) Black Mushroom. When you take it to Adria, she thanks you kindly, and mentions that Pepin needs a demon brain to make some Elixir. If you go talk to him regarding the Black Mushroom quest, Pepin confirms this.

Many gruesome sights await in the labyrinth.

When you return to the dungeon, the next monster you kill yields a brain you should deliver to the Healer. He'll give you a small sample of Elixir, instructing you to carry it to the Witch.

Finally, the Witch berates you for showing up too late with the sample; she no longer has a use for it, and why don't you just keep it?

Using the Spectral Elixir adds two points to each of your Experience characteristics, makes it worth the trouble.

The Anvil of Fury (Group 4: Level 10)

Trigger Character: Griswold the Blacksmith

For the Warrior class, the Anvil of Fury is one of the best quests in the game. This excursion culminates in your acquiring a Unique high-end weapon; Griswold's Edge. While on level 9, visit Griswold and he'll tell you about a mystical Anvil that contains "the very essence" of the demonic underworld.

"Any weapon crafted on this burning anvil is imbued with great power," Griswold tells you. "I may be able to make you a weapon capable of defeating even the darkest lord of hell!"

You'll find the Anvil on Level 10, sitting on a small island in the lava. The entire level is actually centered around this island (if the quest is part of your set), making it the focal point of monster resistance.

To lay hands on the Anvil, clear the perimeter of dungeon denizens first; this process can be tedious and painful. Try to draw the monsters out in smaller groups to take care of business, and take any advantage of narrow walkways that inhibit monster movement. Proceed with caution when you finally make your way to the prize.

If you take the Anvil to Griswold, he'll use it to fashion the impressive "Griswold's Edge" blade. Even non-Warriors may make good use of the blade, though it does come with some negatives that will eventually make a Sorcerer or Rogue consider unloading it for Gold.

THE SLAIN HERO (LEVEL 9)

Single players will come across the body of a Slain Hero while exploring the dungeon's ninth level, and add an item to their inventory that will prove pivotal in the battles just ahead.

In other words, the Slain Hero will help ensure that you have what it takes to face upcoming monsters, just in case luck has been unkind in terms of the spells or armor you've managed to collect at random.

For the Warrior, that means a decent suit of armor. For the Sorcerer, a book of Lightning. The Rogue can expect to lay hands on a high-quality bow.

THE WARLORD OF BLOOD (GROUP 5: LEVEL 13)

Trigger Object: The Steel Tome

Go to Cain after you come across the Steel Tome and he'll tell you about a legendary warrior mentioned in the chronicles of the Sin War. "Stained by a thousand years of war, blood, and death," he says, "the Warlord of Blood stands upon a mountain of his tattered victims. His dark blade screams a black curse to the living, a tortured invitation to any who would stand before this executioner of hell."

Once you've read the book, the stairway between Levels 13 and 14 becomes accessible, and the Warlord will prepare to disembowel you.

Try to clear the level before drawing out the Warlord, paying particular attention to the immediate area around his room. You don't want any of his minions getting in your way. Next to Lazarus, and Diablo himself, the Warlord of Blood is as bad as they come.

Notice that you can draw off the Warlord and then pilfer his treasures; these usually amount to at least one decent suit of armor and some high-end weaponry. If you lead the Warlord off and ditch him in the dungeon, there's only a couple of relatively minor monsters between you and the major trove of the hell levels. Head back to town, sell stuff, buy stuff, stock up—then come back and reacquaint yourself with the Warlord.

If you're playing the Sorcerer or Rogue, keep your distance, or the Warlord of Blood will quite likely slice you in half with a couple of swipes. A Warrior with a serious Armor Class might be able to go toe-to-toe, but watch that Health level: If it drops below half, you'll need to break off and heal up.

If you're packing the Stone Curse Spell, the Warlord is no more intimidating than the average Unique. Stone him, give him two or three whacks, and then turn and run before the spell wears off. You don't want to be standing in front of the Warlord when he gets mobile, so put back some distance the instant the spell begins to wear off.

Keep chipping away, and you'll claim another decent piece of weaponry when the Warlord of Blood goes to meet his maker.

LACHDANAN
(GROUP 5: LEVEL 14)

Trigger Character: Lachdanan

You find Lachdanan trapped on Level 14. He tells you he was once captain of King Leoric's knights, but later succumbed to the mad king's curse. Cain confirms the story of this unfortunate "caught within the grasp of the King's Curse." Lachdanan has not yet submitted to the darkness, but he's fading fast.

"I've heard of a Golden Elixir," Lachdanan tells you, "that could lift the curse and allow my soul to rest, but I have been unable to find it."

It turns out Lachdanan has been looking in the wrong neighborhood: The Golden Elixir actually lies a level lower in the dungeon, in the same room with the large pentagram on the floor. Secure the prize and return with it to Lachdanan, and he rewards you with his helm, the Veil of Steel, as well as another random magic item he drops upon his demise. The Veil is an excellent piece of armor for all classes, though it does come with a -20% Light Radius.

ARCHBISHOP LAZARUS
(ENDGAME: LEVEL 15)

Trigger Item: The Staff of Lazarus

Preparatory to the showdown with Diablo, you must deal with Lazarus. On Level 15, you'll come across a large room with a penta-

gram on the floor. In that vicinity note an apparatus called the Vile Stand, upon which rests the Staff of Lazarus.

Take the staff to Tristram, and show it to Cain. He fills in the rest of the *Diablo* backstory, and sends you back to the depths to confront the Vile Betrayer.

Back in the pentagram room, a red portal—"To The Unholy Altar"—appears.

Through the portal, you arrive in a small, U-shaped set-piece, featuring two large cages of Snow Witches and a couple of Advocates. To enter the Witch cages, stand on the circular areas near the books in the nearby rooms. When you read a book while standing on the ornate circles, you instantly teleport to the nearest Witch pen.

Before reading a book and making the leap, make sure all the doors near the witch pen—doors you've already passed through—are closed again. The witches will run from you, and a closed door makes them much easier to corral.

When you've read both books and disposed of the respective throngs, return to the area where you first appeared in the set-piece. Step on the ornate circle to teleport to Lazarus's chamber.

While Lazarus talks, no one will attack you—not the long-winded priest or any of the other Uniques nearby. Of course, fair is fair: Until the priest finishes his spiel, you won't be able to attack, either.

What you can do, fortunately, is run away.

You're still in the set piece where you read the teleporting books, so the layout should be familiar. Duck around a corner, and let Lazarus finish talking. If you stand in the center of the room, a nasty ambush ensues when the priest finishes his oration, and that's generally not a very healthy way to start the fight.

Duck off down one of the halls while Lazarus speaks, and you'll find you're out of the "trigger zone" for the monsters. They'll simply stand and wait for you to return, and then pursue you down a hallway. That's generally a much easier battle from your standpoint then fighting the horde from the center of that large room.

Further, if you took some advice and closed the nearby doors before fighting the Snow Witches, the crowd pursuing you can do a lot less milling around when it catches up. Continue to fall back and chip away when you need a healing break. Lazarus doesn't pursue you; he just lingers in the large chamber until you've finished with the crowd.

Fighting the evil priest with magic can be a painful experience: He'll dish Fireballs in your direction as you unload your favorite spell. If your best attack is a magic one, hopefully it's Stone Curse or Elemental—something with an added aspect that's defensive in nature, allowing you to do some damage without taking a disproportionate amount in return.

As the Rogue, with no one to bother you but Lazarus, you can rush at him, forcing him to teleport, and then target the area where he'll rematerialize (watch the light patterns on the floor) and unload a volley of arrows. As long as he doesn't go too far, you can keep him off-balance this way. Eventually he succumbs.

As the Warrior, things can get a little dicey. If you don't have any high-end magic to speak of, you'll be reduced to healing yourself, and rushing around at Lazarus as he teleports. Again, watch the light patterns on the floor—follow the fiend even while he's in mid-teleport—and be waiting when he shows up. Usually, you can land a forceful blow, and your proximity will compel Lazarus to teleport again. Stay nimble, and ready to heal whenever the need arises.

Of course, Lazarus and his minions spit up some serious treasure, giving you the last good chunk of resources at your disposal before the final showdown.

DIABLO (ENDGAME: LEVEL 16)

Once you've disposed of Lazarus, another red portal opens in the room where you arrived at "The Unholy Altar" set-piece. This takes you back to Level 15, where the large pentagram now glows. In the center is a teleporter "Down to Diablo."

Level 16 comprises four quadrants. Advocates and Blood Knights guard the first, open, area. A switch within this area opens the second quadrant. A switch there opens the third quadrant, where two switches open the final section of the dungeon—and the game.

As you arrive at Level 16, you have a couple of options. The open quadrant area, in the upper portion of the map, is a battle royale. Hallways encircle the three other quadrants, and in those halls you'll also find Advocates and Blood Knights, although not in nearly the numbers you'll find within each primary area when it's unsealed.

It's prudent to circle the three sealed quadrants first, clearing out those monsters. When you storm the first quadrant, you must eventually retreat from the onslaught. Leading a line of Knights down one of those hallways, properly emptied ahead of time, can be a very effective way to turn the tables. Try Wall of Fire, or, better yet, Flame Wave.

The first and third hubs are the toughest, as the monster horde tends to notice you all at once. If you have a Scroll of Apocalypse (or two or three), now's the time. By creeping up to those

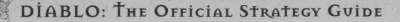

encounter areas, you can at least draw off the Dark Lords, and then return to deal with the Advocates. The Advocates will resist leaving their area, but often that's a good thing: By moving erratically near the doorways, one or two will eventually teleport into the large outer area. The more you can draw out in this fashion, the better it will be for you when you must finally venture into hostile territory. Prepare to heal, and crank up those magical resistances to the best of your ability.

In the third quadrant, you must throw both switches to open Diablo's lair. (Throwing one switch won't release any of the monsters, just in case it occurs to you.)

The good news is that if you're playing the Warrior class, and you've done a good job of collecting armor, Diablo is dust. Sure, he'll occasionally seize the initiative as you pound on him, but keep healing, and keep hacking. As long as your Durability and Fire Resistance are high, the dark one is going to drop.

The Rogue also gets off easy, as long as she has decent fire resistance and a bow to fight with. Simply stay out of the way, and chip at him from a distance, healing when the need arrises.

The Sorcerer can be in some serious trouble. Diablo isn't entirely immune to Magic, but he's resistant enough to eliminate many options (and forget about Stone Curse). Add to that the fact that the big guy is tossing off tremendous Fireballs that can really hamper a Sorcerer's ability to cast Magic, and things get ugly in a hurry.

First, as a Sorcerer, you'll want to draw Diablo off into another part of the level by leading him down a hallway where he can be your only target.

You'll find that each time you throw a spell at Diablo, he may or may not be immune to it. If he's immune (or highly resistant) the spell will pass through him or simply bounce off. In a nutshell, it's hard for the Sorcerer to expend Mana on such a dicey proposition and still heal himself during the battle. If you brought a big, scary magical staff with you, now's the time to use it. At least that allows you to devote your Mana to healing.

If you brought a bow, that can be even better. You need to do some damage to Diablo, and Magic just isn't the best offense. Physical damage always counts, and doing it from a distance is the least painful way.

For all the classes, having a fast-attack weapon or some item that imbues the fastest recovery from attack is a huge help when it comes to dealing with Diablo. Even at that, you have to work on your specific timing so that the demon's attacks don't upset your own. If you fall into such a pattern, break off the assault and rejoin it to try and seize the initiative.

Notice that Diablo's Magic attack, unlike other creatures,' actually affects your armor's Durability. You can only take so much punishment before things start deteriorating.

As far as healing goes, consider using the Healing Scrolls, as opposed to potions. You can hotkey a scroll, and they cast almost instantly, without, of course, drawing off any Mana.

If you find that, no matter what, as a Sorcerer you keep getting your head handed to you, you might consider dumping some stash to get a decent suit of armor, preferably with some kind of fast-attack benefit. That way, you might be able to stand toe-to-toe with the Father of Sin. Hopefully with Mana Shield in effect, and cut him down to size.

GAME OVER

With the fall of Diablo, there remains only one thing to do: Set up the sequel.

Let's just say the ending cinematic is worth the price of admission, although you might have reconsidered this whole "Let's go hunt down Diablo" thing if someone had told you beforehand what a headache it was going to be. . . .

The red pentagram marks the final quest.

9

BATTLE.NET

As enthralling as *Diablo* is in single-player mode, being able to join a band of adventurers below the town of Tristram adds an even deeper dimension.

Most of the tactics and tendencies you acquired as a single player translate directly to multiplayer mode, but some aspects of composing a party and clearing a room bear closer examination.

Due to the diverse nature and significant advantages of each character class, consider always including one of each character type in a party. (Three types and four slots, of course, leaves one to fill.) Indulge yourself.

MULTIPLAYER FEATURES

There are a handful of features in *Diablo* that only activate in the multiplayer game, and some standard features that carry expanded meaning within the multiplayer structure. Aside from just looking at the nuances of group combat or defense, recognizing and properly utilizing *Diablo*'s multiplayer features can greatly enhance your enjoyment, and significantly improve your character's chances for survival.

JOINING A GAME

A multiplayer game of Diablo can be joined in progress at any time, as long as there is an open slot available. The wildfire success of Blizzard's own Battle.net means that games fill up almost as fast as they are created, so don't be shy about creating your own if there's nothing on the Battle.net menu that suits your fancy.

TIP

WHAT ARE MY OFFERS?

TIRED OF SELLING THAT GREAT MAGICAL ITEM FOR A FRACTION OF ITS WORTH TO GRISWOLD OR ADRIA? BLIZZARD'S BATTLE.NET HAS A CENTRAL LOCATION WHERE LARGE NUMBERS OF CHARACTERS CAN CONGREGATE TO BUY AND SELL ITEMS FOR WHATEVER THE MARKET WILL BEAR.

Also, note that you'll begin a joined game in Tristram, though you can send messages to other players currently exploring deep in the dungeon. Thus alerted, the party can cast a Town Portal spell, which you can use to travel directly to their location.

SAVING A GAME

As a multiplayer game of *Diablo* is underway, the characters are constantly being saved. As long as you quit out of a game without being killed, your character will start its next adventure in the exact same condition as when you quit the previous game.

DEATH OF A MULTIPLAYER

As with any noble adventurer, your multiplayer *Diablo* character may one day be faced with insurmountable odds or outright treachery, resulting in an untimely demise. Death in the multiplayer world carries with it some particular nuances, which you should note ahead of time.

DEATH BY MONSTER

Whenever a player is killed by a monster, every item currently equipped, as well as half the player's gold, winds up lying on the dungeon floor. The player can then rejoin the game, assuming no one is going to be so kind as to perform a Resurrection, and set about reclaiming the lost goods.

Of course, other players might gather the loot for themselves in the mean time, but that aside the treasure will be left where it was dropped.

If you choose to rejoin the game without quitting—the "Restart in Town" option—you'll have one point each of Health and Mana to work with upon your rebirth, and the same loss of items still applies.

PLAYER FRIENDLY VS. PLAYER ATTACK

The small button near your Mana globe in multiplayer toggles between "Player Friendly" and "Player Attack" modes, determining whether or not another player character can be targeted and attacked with a hand-held weapon.

In "Player Friendly," you can still damage friends with an arrow gone astray or an errant magical attack, but you can stand shoulder-to-shoulder and whack monster without having to worry about mistaking your buddy for a target.

Now Hear This

One final note on the general multiplayer interface, concerning the dastardly nature of characters whose sole purpose is to raid ongoing games by slaying lesser characters to claim treasure off the corpses. . . .

In order to combat this deviance, the boys at Blizzard made it so that the most a player can get for killing another is half of the slain character's gold. And an ear.

The reason is that, occasionally, one of these evil characters builds up such a bad reputation in multiplayer circles that an actual bounty is offered for his head.

Of course, lugging a head around can be bothersome, and a real downer at most social occasions, so Blizzard settled for an ear. The ear is collected as proof of a certain character's demise—it bears the character's name as proof—and is generally accepted as the only acceptable means of claiming a bounty.

The Classes in Multiplayer

In single-player mode, even the heartiest fighter or most magical Sorcerer must, to a certain extent, be a diverse character, at least as much as its class allows. Though the same strategy serves well in multiplayer, it's possible to specialize further. Hopefully, other members of the party will always be there to handle tasks ill-suited to your character.

THE WARRIOR

Yes, the Warrior is still going to be down there in the trenches, slugging it out with the evil hordes, but now he's going to have a little help. Of all the traits a Warrior might devalue, the first is probably Magic. With a properly configured party of heroes, there's bound to be others more adept, and the fighter should fork over any decent Spellbooks to the Sorcerer of his choice.

Accentuate Strength and Dexterity, and look for magical items that enhance those traits, as well as Vitality. Also, fast hit recovery is something to covet, as is significant magic resistance. Not only does that help you out when you're battling the legions of hell, but some Sorcerers tend to be loose cannons, and as a Warrior you'll spend a lot of time in the line of fire.

THE SORCERER

Just as the Warrior can now set aside his magical inclinations, the Sorcerer has little need of Strength in multiplayer. Almost any armor will do, and because the damage a Sorcerer inflicts comes from Magic, what use is Strength?

Pour those points into Magic, and look for items that detract from the Damage a monster does in combat to further heighten your defenses. Also, look for offensive spells that don't carry a blast-radius component (that is, those that don't explode). Notice that the higher-level spells tend to allow you to focus Fire or Lightning into smaller areas, which is a skill to covet. Take pains to avoid damaging your partners, lest they take exception.

The Rogue

While the Sorcerer provides the magical component to a party's distance attack, the Rogue employs the bow to add a physical component. As with the other classes, your primary trait should be the advantage you lean on in combat.

Strength is somewhat important (you need good Strength to use a bow, as you would for any other large weapon). Beyond that, when you're not pouring points into Dexterity, go with Vitality. Look for bows that carry a magical component—not only in characteristic

Tip

The multiplayer universe includes only a few quests: "The Butcher," "The Skeleton King," "The Vile Betrayer," and the endgame. None of these is set up on an extra level, and only the endgame requires a trigger. Once you reach Level 14, send someone up to town to talk with Deckard Cain; when he returns, Diablo and his minions will be waiting on the Pentagram.

adjustments but those that include fire or lightning as part of the damage they do.

SPECIAL SKILLS IN MULTIPLAYER

By including all three character types in a party of adventurers, you have the ability to recharge staffs, repair worn Durability, and disarm any traps.

The disarming technique is simple: No one opens a chest until the Rogue checks it first. The Rogue can have a simple term for this—"Clear" or some such thing—that lets everyone know that the chests

TIP

LIGHT MY WAY

IF ONE AMONG YOUR PARTY HAS AN OBJECT THAT INCREASES LIGHT RADIUS, EVERYONE NEARBY WILL ENJOY THAT ADVANTAGE. IF ANYONE HAS A SPARE FINGER, EQUIPPING A RING WITH THE PROPER MAGICAL COMPONENT MAKES EVERYONE'S LIFE A LITTLE EASIER. DON'T KEEP SUCH AN ITEM UNUSED IN YOUR INVENTORY IF SOMEONE CAN UTILIZE IT.

in that room have been investigated. The Rogue bears a certain responsibility here, because she must discover every chest before giving the word, and sometimes chests can be hidden in corners or up against walls.

The Sorcerer and the Warrior can employ their specific skills to repair or recharge weapons, armor, or staffs. Simply have one character throw down an item and another pick it up to perform the service.

Of course, this method "wears down" items over time, as opposed to repairs or recharges done in Tristram. Deep in the dungeon, however, you'll appreciate a diverse party.

MULTIPLAYER EXPLORATION AND COMBAT

Scouring the dungeon with a group of characters is done a little differently than in single-player mode, though the basic components remain unchanged. Your character benefits from having other characters nearby who possess skills you thus no longer need concern yourself with. The essence of cooperative play is allowing other characters to do what they do best, and to perform your own tasks to the best of your ability.

In a single-player game, you can occasionally afford to get bored or restless. You can't afford that luxury in multiplayer, as a reckless player inevitably is left lying on the dungeon floor by his disgusted comrades.

For exploration purposes, regardless of the characters in your party, but assuming there's at least one of each type, consider these roles in addition to performing your special skill for other party members.

- Warrior: opens doors, patrols near portals
- Sorcerer: throws magic at large groups
- Rogue: concentrates bow on major monsters from a distance

With these roles in mind, effectively coordinating a combat sequence makes up most of a multiplayer game. Most single-player tactics still apply, though there are some distinct advantages to group warfare.

OFFENSIVE TACTICS

With each of the character classes specializing a little more than in the single-player mode, offensive tactics for a group of adventurers place a premium on coordination, and also contingency plans. Eventually, someone is going to go down in battle, and a good Plan B is essential to making sure the entire party doesn't follow suit.

There are four basic environments that you'll encounter in the dungeon, each of which merits particular tactical consideration from the group standpoint. They are the large room, the small room, the wide hall, and the narrow hall.

Of course, some locations combine various aspects of those four broad categories, but thinking about occupied space in those four ways provides a good basis for tactics that you can tailor to a variety of situations.

As with the single-player game, forcing the monsters to attack through the narrowest avenue is the safest way to go. It's just that now you have a group of players jockeying for position, and you want to make sure that everyone can attack effectively, without exposing their character or their partners to undue risk.

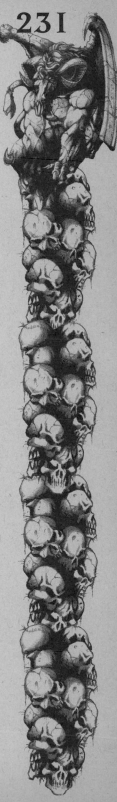

Tip

The four gates into the labyrinth work differently in Battle.net. In single-player mode, additional entrances open at the beginning of each level; in Battle.net, someone in your party must achieve a certain Character Level before additional portals will present themselves. The church is always open to Level 1; the mausoleum doorway into Level 5 opens when someone's achieved Character Level 8; the cave entrance opens when someone reaches Character Level 14, and the crevasse opens when someone hits Character Level 17.

Small Room

Imagine, if you will, a doorway in a wide hall. The smallish room on the other side presents the easiest tactical situation for a party of adventurers to surmount.

To one side of the door stands the Warrior. Directly in front of the door stands the Sorcerer. Farther down the hall (some 25 feet relatively) waits the Rogue.

The Sorcerer opens the door and cuts loose with Inferno or some form of Lightning—three or four bursts that incinerate most of the demons waiting just inside the room, and certainly any close enough to damage the Sorcerer while the spells are being cast. Then the Sorcerer turns and runs from the open door, taking up a position near the Rogue.

As the monsters, looking dazed and feeling significantly warmer than a few seconds earlier, emerge into the hall, the Warrior taps them on the shoulder once or twice—with an axe.

Startled and engaged, a monster freezes in the doorway, blocking the egress of its brethren. Any of the Warrior's weapons that don't fall quickly feel the added pain of the Rogue's arrows. If the hall is wide enough, or the spell precise enough, the Sorcerer can continue to attack. The key, of course, is evaluating the chance of doing damage to the Warrior.

Once monsters stop emerging from the room, it's likely there will be some with ranged attacks remaining inside. Since you can count on them firing a concentrated volley at the door, the Warrior gets the unenviable task of leading the charge. Have the other characters close to the door, so that the Warrior isn't all alone for long. Let the Warrior give the signal to advance.

Most monsters with ranged attacks won't stand in one place if you run toward them. And when they're running, they can't attack. Thus, the Warrior charges the throng, but more with the intention of herding them than closing the gap and engaging one foe. The object is to gather the monsters, so that the Sorcerer and Rogue, hot on the Warrior's heals, can dish out some damage to the milling crowd: The

mage uses some wide-ranging Magic while the Rogue concentrates on either Unique monsters or those which are engaged in attacking a member of the party. If the Warrior rushes down one side of the room towards the distance attackers, they'll crowd into the other half to set up and open fire. Once they're headed in that direction, attention focused momentarily on the onrushing Warrior, it's a relatively simple matter for the Sorcerer to advance halfway down the room opposite the Warrior's position, and blast away. The Rogue enters last, and opens fire on any monster still able to mount a counter-offensive.

LARGE ROOM

Entering a large area with a party of adventurers presents some unique challenges, since most large areas are comprised of several encounter zones, where monsters are triggered when someone comes within a certain proximity.

For this reason, it's essential that the party stays relatively close together. If four players enter a large room and fan out, rest assured that every monster in the joint will notice. The idea is to overwhelm the party, and your mission, tactically speaking, is to avoid giving the monsters that chance.

Decide beforehand which wall you're going to stick to. If anyone has a scroll of Infravision, it can be particularly useful when entering a large area. You'll be able to judge the initial position of the monsters, and also see those knots of bad guys waiting for someone to wander into their immediate area. Watch out that you don't roust them with errant projectiles.

Of course, if the monsters can be drawn out of the room or area through a narrow avenue, the job gets a lot easier. You might even consider having the Rogue, because of the speed of her ranged attack, stir up the room and lead everyone back out into an ambush.

But assume that the monsters aren't cooperating, or that you're in the Caverns, where there are often too many monsters and too much space to make such a tactic reasonable.

The key is to find a relatively defensible area—not a suicide dead-end or a corner—and then draw the monsters into that area a little at a time. In the same way that a Warrior generally attacks in single-player—whacking and then dropping back when the monsters threaten to overwhelm, a few monsters at a time can be drawn towards the rest of the party. At a predetermined point in the ensuing chase, the Warrior steps up and holds the monsters for a brief instant. The Rogue opens up with the Bow on the monster closest to the Warrior, as the Warrior falls back out of the line of fire. Finally, as the monsters' attention is momentarily divided between the Rogue and the Warrior, the Sorcerer steps up with some crowd-pleasing magic. Hopefully, enough damage is done that the Warrior can re-enter the fray at that point, polishing off the weakened monsters before they can react to the situation. Be sure to have a predetermined number of attacks (or kills) for the Sorcerer, so the Warrior can rush forward just as the last spell fades.

WIDE HALLWAY

The wide hallway is a killing zone in multiplayer, as it affords each member of the group a chance to concentrate fire on a portal through which all monsters must pass.

The consideration here is that you actually want to fight in the

hallway, as opposed to entering whatever room is on the other side. Usually, that's because there are two types of formidable monsters present—one which will pursue and one type which will stay in the room. The most obvious example is the presence of Advocates and Death Knights.

The key, of course, is to jam the monsters up at the door, using the Warrior to engage each foe as it emerges. For the purpose of spellcasting, the Sorcerer should be off to the same side of the hall as the Warrior, so that any magic gone astray has a lesser chance of damaging the partner.

The Rogue, with a much more precise method of delivering damage, can stand virtually anywhere that affords a good shot. The key is that magical monsters with distance attacks may be shooting past the onrushing horde, and they'll draw a bead if anyone stays in one place too long. The Warrior, up against the wall on one side of the door, should be safe from such harassment.

By concentrating fire on each enemy as it emerges, the party can effectively mow down monsters, even the tougher ones, before they can do more then take a whack or two at the Warrior. He should be up to it.

If the Sorcerer leads the attack, drawing foes to the same side of the hall as the Warrior, the Warrior can take a swipe without stepping too far out in front of the doorway, and at that point the monster should stop and begin to attack the Warrior in earnest. By that time, that one monster has already suffered a Magic attack, a blow or two from the Warrior, and the Rogue has been peppering it with arrows the whole time. It's about to die.

Narrow Hallway

One of the most perplexing tasks in multiplayer is conquering a narrow hallway. Often, there's just no good way to fit three or four characters into a small space like a narrow hall and still have them fight effectively, especially if you're thinking about using magic.

Tactically, how you assault a narrow hall varies depending whether or not there's a door at the end, whether the monsters at the end of the hallway will pursue, and whether or not they have ranged attacks.

Pursuing monsters without ranged attacks are playthings for the Sorcerer, since spells like Wall of Fire and Flame Wave can make any narrow passage almost unsurvivable. The following example assumes the hall is two characters wide.

Have the Rogue enter the room or otherwise attract the attention of the monsters. The Sorcerer waits outside in the hall, spell at the ready. Directly behind him waits a Warrior.

The Rogue draws out the opposition, running past the Sorcerer, who then opens up with serious magic. The monsters are taking damage, but it's obvious they'll reach the Sorcerer before dying off completely.

As they close the gap, the Warrior steps from behind the Sorcerer, flanking the mage. The Sorcerer turns and flees down the hallway as the first of the monsters encounters the Warrior. The monsters are weak and the hall is narrow, so the Warrior can go toe-to-toe for a few seconds, especially with the Rogue lending support from a short distance. The Sorcerer retreats past the Rogue, turns, and readies his spells once more. When the foremost monster falls to the Warrior, the Warrior falls back, following the Rogue to positions behind the Sorcerer. In this way, the characters can leap frog down the narrow passage, taking turns in attacking and keeping the monsters at bay.

A Final Word on Offense

Variations on these themes are legion, influenced by your characters' relative health, their Magic resistance, and the resistance of the monsters involved.

You must develop a strategy for standard monsters, and an alternative for those with ranged attacks. Combining the two types merely involves combining the methods you conclude are most effective.

Finally, remember that *Diablo* evolves, and its characters develop continually. Even if a strategy works fine for your group, don't be afraid to experiment when new items or spells present new opportunities. Eventually, new and stronger foes will require you to make strategic adjustments. If you've taken time to experiment with diverse attack modes, you'll burn a lot less coin of the realm on Resurrect Scrolls.

Defensive Considerations

Just as it's crucial to have a solid plan of offense for your party, where everyone has a relatively clear set of responsibilities in a given situation, it's also important to consider some defensive tactics. Of course, where *Diablo* is concerned, "defense" is a very kind word. Each character is largely responsible for their own defense, in the form of magical resistances and the ability to heal on the run.

The most basic aspect of group defense is simply how to keep from being overwhelmed, and what the plan of action is should a horde of monsters manage to kill one of your group, and/or splinter the party.

As with the single player game, the key is not to flee into unknown territory, and to actually anticipate a fall-back position that affords a tactical advantage. The best places to defend tactically are somewhat different in multiplayer, and dependent entirely on the composition of your party.

Whether you use the foregoing offensive tactics as a framework for your own endeavors, or develop a strategy tailored exclusively to your group of characters, you're bound to hit on one eventually that really does the trick. With each successive level of dungeon, you'll modify your favorite attack to better suit the environment, but your best mode of group attack will probably change radically only a few times throughout the game, as new spells and weapons are introduced into the mix.

As you explore each level, passing through each new room and hallway, communicate. Have everyone call up the map when you think you notice a prime ambush area, and have everyone take note: This is our fallback position.

Then, instead of a random panic when those Death Knights start pouring from a wide portal, you simply fall back—ideally leading the monsters through some confined space where they can't overrun you through sheer force of numbers.

As with your offensive tactics, realize that the introduction of new spells or weapons can influence the most effective fall-back ambush strategy. Though it's not nearly as glamorous as devising cruel and unusual methods of attack, take a few minutes following any discussion of altering the offensive gameplan, and analyze briefly if there are significant defensive implications as a result of some new insight.

IO

THE MAKING OF DIABLO

An Interview with the Devils Behind the Game

When I walked into the offices, the lights were off in the reception area and the blinds were drawn. My eyes adjusted to the darkened room. There was no receptionist at the desk, just the posterior of a 17-inch monitor angled toward the door. Thinking I'd come to the wrong place, I turned to go, but I stopped when I heard a recent, familiar sound—that unforgettable claw-hammer-meets-ripe-cantaloupe splurch meaning someone or something has just been disemboweled. I was in the right place.

"Just a second," someone said sweetly from behind the monitor. "Whoa! Haven't seen her before. I think this is the Succubus. Hmm, I'll be right with you."—Tap, tap, tap—splurch. "Got her!"

During the tense weeks before *Diablo* hit the shelves, it seemed as though everyone at Blizzard was playing the game. Whenever I called to beg for technical assistance or whine that I hadn't seen the absolutely latest version, invariably I had to wait while the person on the other end of line saved a game in progress. The lights were dimmed, as they had been for months to reduce computer screen glare, when I arrived to interview *Diablo*'s creators. Most of the people I saw wore that distant, bleary-eyed look that one gets from too much road time on a PC, glare or no glare. They looked like a bunch of long-haul truckers rolling up to the end of the line.

"We ask for lots of input around here," Eric Schaefer told me. The lead designer and commanding artist-in-residence is a big, friendly, goateed guy who looks like he spends a great deal of time glued to his computer. "Everybody's playing the game constantly, and they're free to speak their minds about what they like and don't like. It really keeps us on our toes."

"Yeah, right now we're playing it all the time," agreed Schaefer's partner in crime, David Brevik. "At this point, basically, we're just trying to make it better." The lead programmer on the project is wrapped a little tighter than his colleague today; he's been dealing with the last of the game's bugs all night long. You can almost see lines of code skittering across his eyeballs.

Diablo's cocreators met while working at a series of small Silicon Valley game companies. Brevik worked on a number of PC-to-console conversions. Schaefer started out doing clip art, but soon found himself creating game graphics.

"We called up Dave and said 'Hey, do want to start a company?'" Schaefer recalls. In 1993, he and his bother Max, also an artist, joined with Brevik and founded Condor. Their first contract was to create a Sega Genesis version of *Justice League Task Force*.

But what they really wanted to do was design PC games.

"That's what we usually play on our own time," Schaefer says. "The games we wanted to play were almost always on the PC."

Brevik adds, "We wanted to create some complex, challenging games that wouldn't necessarily do well in an arcade—games for guys like us, and maybe a little younger, but not for kids."

They got their chance in 1994 at the Comdex show in Las Vegas. As they continued work on the Genesis version of *Justice League*, a Southern California-based company called Blizzard worked on the game's Super NES version.

"We were talking with the Blizzard guys at the show," Brevik says, "and they were telling us about this really cool pre-alpha version of a

game they had been working on called *Warcraft*. Later, we talked on the phone, and I tried to get a prerelease version of the game, because I was very interested in playing it."

During that conversation Brevik also learned that Blizzard was looking for PC developers to expand its line.

"I told them, we've got some great ideas right here," he says. "Why don't you come up and listen to one? They did, and we pitched them *Diablo*, and they loved it."

Meanwhile, *Warcraft: Orcs and Humans* had just been released and with the (as yet unknown) incredible success of *Warcraft II: Tides of Darkness* still in its infancy, Blizzard was looking for ways to expand into new gaming territory.

"They said their game would be *Rogue*, *Moira*, and *NetHack* meet *Crusader: No Remorse* and *DOOM*," Producer Bill Roper says. "Now that was something different. We all loved the old Unix-based games, and when we took a look at the design documents, we just had to go with it."

During most of *Diablo's* development, Condor operated as an independent entity. Then, about six months before the game's release, Condor became Blizzard North.

"They (Blizzard) said all along that if things went well, in a couple of games, maybe we could think about coming into the fold," Brevik says. "But *Diablo* was coming along so well they picked us up. We're really happy with our relationship."

"We knew that if we didn't grab them," continues Roper, "that when *Diablo* shipped, somebody else would. In the process of putting this game out, we have become a big family."

The buzz about this game was deafening long before anyone would actually hear the splurch of zombie guts on a cold labyrinth floor. As the project moved along, game magazines wondered at Blizzard's chutzpah in bringing out a new RPG—a new, unpredictable market at best—instead of following up with a *Warcraft III*. Kids in parking lots started arguing about whether *Diablo* or *Ultima Online* would be the better multiplayer network game. Netizens speculated endlessly about the game in Internet chat rooms.

"In our local CompUSA," Brevik says, "the store managers had mocked up their own little stand for *Diablo*. They'd cut out clippings from magazines, blown them up, and pasted them together: 'Preorder *Diablo* here.' It was totally amazing to me."

Brevik and Schaefer had kicked around the idea for a different type of role-playing game from Condor's founding. Brevik was a long-time fan of the old Unix-based games, those simple dungeon hacks that were different every time you played them. "It was all text," Brevik says, "so you were really just moving the squiggle around to fight the letter 'A.' Not all that exciting. But we thought, what if we gave them a graphic treatment?"

So the two devoted gamers pursued the idea of a random-environment, dungeon exploration game with a 3-D graphical look.

"We were basically coming up with a game we'd like to play," Brevik says.

"Most of the role-playing stuff on the market at the time tended to be along the lines of adventures and epic quests, which we weren't really looking for," says Schaefer. "We originally wanted a fun game that let you sit down at night and blow off some steam for a little while, hacking up monsters. It developed into much more than what we started with."

The original idea was to develop a "turn-based" game much like the old Unix-based games (or chess, for that matter): Players would

move a character one square, and then the opponent or monster would move one square. Eight months into the development, the folks at Blizzard suggested making *Diablo* a real-time game, like *Warcraft II*.

"We resisted and pushed for a turn-based game," Schaefer says, "And they said OK to that, which I think was pretty cool of them. But then the real fight started up here."

"We had this big argument in Eric's kitchen," Brevik recalls. "We stomped around, dug our heels in and said, 'We're not changing it!' From an art standpoint, it would really have been no different, but from a programming standpoint, it was going to be a big pain for me. But then we thought about it some more and decided to try their idea. I hacked up something in a couple of days to see what it would be like, and we all just loved it."

Brevik had to develop a new engine to run the game in real time, but it added an element of almost *DOOM*-like action that made the game unique among RPGs. Schaefer says that although they were sold on the game's real-time aspect, they still wanted to make the play different than a game like *Warcraft*.

They also wanted a different look for more than 150 monsters populating *Diablo's* dungeons—an unprecedented number in an industry where other developers brag about 10.

"We didn't really want the traditional role-playing monsters," Schaefer says. "No dragons, elves, orcs, trolls, and such. We leaned toward the more demonic and undead type of monsters to give the game a creepier feel."

"We felt that orcs and elves were well situated in our *Warcraft* universe," adds Roper "and that *Diablo* would give us all a chance to explore the darker side of gothic horror and fantasy."

Along with a chance to hack up these dark creatures, Blizzard wanted to include the element of role-playing they all loved. To do this they developed the surface quests.

"They were such a good role-playing element," Schaefer says, "but at first we didn't really know what to do with them. They weren't integrated into the game very well. It was a little too free-form in the beginning: You could complete quests or not. Then we all really sat down to develop the storyline."

Changing the way that the quests fit into the game altered *Diablo* significantly. What had been little more than a highly sophisticated monster hunt was becoming a far more sophisticated RPG with a strong narrative element. The more that they tweaked it, the closer the game came to delivering the best of both worlds.

Then Battle.net broke the mold.

"Again," Brevik says, "the multiplayer capability was just another way to make the game better. It allowed us to add a whole new dimension and lots of new possibilities."

Everyone realized that network support was essential to realizing the games potential, and the added introduction of Blizzard's Internet gaming service Battle.net pushed that concept over the top.

"Offering our customers a simple and free way to get together and hunt down *Diablo* over the Internet was a huge decision," says Roper. "We knew that we would, in reality, be shipping two products in one by putting out *Diablo* and Battle.net in the same box. But once the idea was formed, we were all too dedicated to making it a reality to do anything but make it happen."

The final version of *Diablo* utilizes nearly 5,000 frames of animation for the heroes, more than any other game on the market (as of this writing). *Ultima VIII*, by comparison, uses about 2,000 frames. Why take the time to draw and digitize so many different looks for the heroes?

"Because when I pick up an axe," Schaefer says "I want it to look like an axe. I think other people care about that kind of thing too. It just looks better."

Diablo also contains a lot of original "mood music" created by composer Matt Uelmen. The game's distinctive background score is one of the spookier, more disturbing elements, adding much to the overall experience.

But if one element sets *Diablo* apart, it is its randomness. The game system was designed to randomly generate the layout of each new level, with unpredictable attacks and a wide variety of unpredictable attackers.

"That's probably what I like best about the game," Brevik says. "I can almost guarantee there are no commercially licensed graphic RPGs out there that are replayable in the same way this game is. I'm very proud of that."

"The fact that every time you play *Diablo* you are getting a new and unique gaming experience is what keeps me playing even after all the testing," adds Roper. "The character classes all play very differently, and you just never know what you'll find next."

"We're never satisfied," Schaefer says. "We push each other to make things better and better. We do things over and over again. We render the same character five times, and we still don't like it. Sometimes the guys get mad, but in the long run, it makes a better game."

"We may be only making a computer game," Brevik says, "but we have very high standards. I still think we could improve this game."

That was back before *Diablo* was fully cooked, and I can report from personal observation that the versions that followed my interview were, indeed, better and better and better.

Before I left, I stopped off to visit one last time at the reception

desk. I had this idea about stealing some tips on the way out. It was dark in the hallway, and I got turned around on my way—but then I just followed my ears: Tap, tap, tap—splurch.

"Gotcha!"

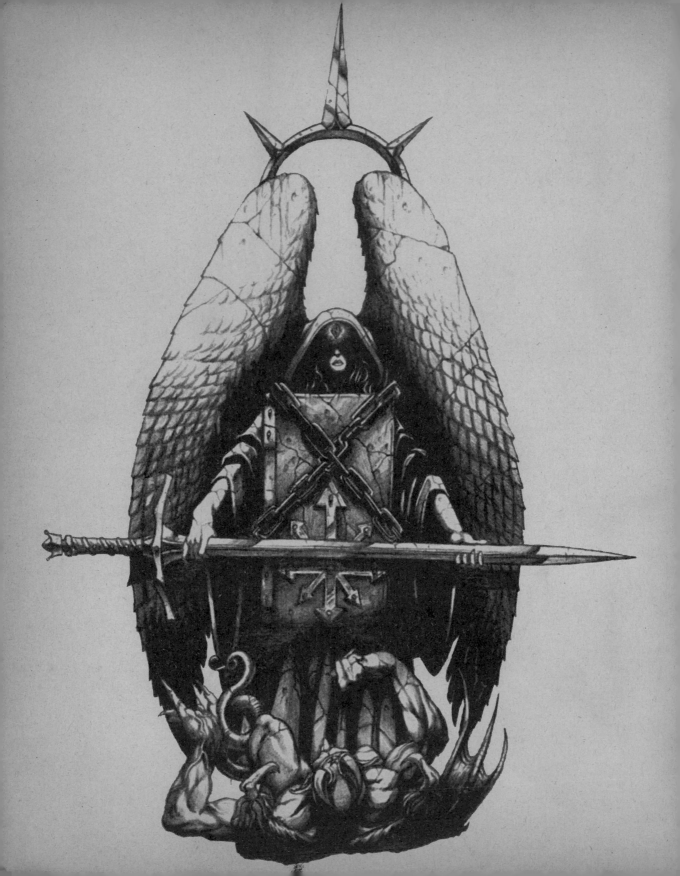

To Order Books

Please send me the following items:

Quantity	Title	Unit Price	Total
_____	_____	$ _____	$ _____
_____	_____	$ _____	$ _____
_____	_____	$ _____	$ _____
_____	_____	$ _____	$ _____
_____	_____	$ _____	$ _____

Subtotal $ _____

Deduct 10% when ordering 3-5 books $ _____

7.25% Sales Tax (CA only) $ _____

8.25% Sales Tax (TN only) $ _____

5.0% Sales Tax (MD and IN only) $ _____

Shipping and Handling* $ _____

Total Order $ _____

Shipping and Handling depend on Subtotal.

Subtotal	Shipping/Handling
$0.00–$14.99	$3.00
$15.00–$29.99	$4.00
$30.00–$49.99	$6.00
$50.00–$99.99	$10.00
$100.00–$199.99	$13.50
$200.00+	Call for Quote

Foreign and all Priority Request orders:
Call Order Entry department
for price quote at 916/632-4400

This chart represents the total retail price of books only
(before applicable discounts are taken).

By Telephone: With MC or Visa, call 800-632-8676, 916-632-4400. Mon-Fri, 8:30-4:30.
WWW {http://www.primapublishing.com}

Orders Placed Via Internet E-mail {sales@primapub.com}

By Mail: Just fill out the information below and send with your remittance to:

Prima Publishing
P.O. Box 1260BK
Rocklin, CA 95677

My name is _____

I live at _____

City _____ State _____ Zip _____

MC/Visa# _____ Exp. _____

Check/Money Order enclosed for $ _____ Payable to Prima Publishing

Daytime Telephone _____

Signature _____